THE GREAT
WORLD WAR II ES

CW00825791

BRITISH PRISONERS OF WAR IN ITALY: PATHS TO FREEDOM

ESCAPE AND EVASION IN WARTIME ITALY

MALCOLM TUDOR

EMILIA PUBLISHING

New edition first published in
Great Britain in 2012 by

EMILIA PUBLISHING
Woodlands, Bryn Gardens, Newtown,
Powys, SY16 2DR

www.emiliapublishing.com

emiliapublishing@btinternet.com

Copyright © 2012 Malcolm Tudor

Malcolm Tudor has asserted his moral rights
to be identified as the author

A CIP catalogue of this book is available
from the British Library

ISBN 978-0-9538964-7-9

Cover designed and typeset in Bembo 11pt
by Chandler Book Design
www.chandlerbookdesign.co.uk

Printed and bound by
the MPG Books Group in the UK

CONTENTS

Other books by Malcolm Tudor:

At War in Italy 1943-1945:
True Adventures in Enemy Territory

Beyond the Wire:
A True Story of Allied POWs in Italy 1943-1945

Escape from Italy 1943-45:
Allied Escapers and Helpers in Fascist Italy

Prisoners and Partisans:
Escape and Evasion in World War II Italy

SOE in Italy 1940-1945:
The Real Story

Special Force:
SOE and the Italian Resistance 1943-1945

The books on World War II Italy cover British and
Allied prisoners of war, escape and evasion, special operations,
air supply and Resistance.

For full information and online ordering, please visit the
Emilia Publishing website: www.emiliapublishing.com

Also available through UK booksellers
and Amazon Marketplace

*To: The Allied Forces and
their helpers in Italy, 1940-1945.*

ACKNOWLEDGEMENTS

I would like to thank the former prisoners of war in
Italy, the Italians, their relatives and everyone who has
provided me with information and practical help.

Special thanks to Gaetano Avogadri; The Guarnieri
family; Hugh Rees; Doctor Oreste Scaglioni; Luigi
Sesenna; Eileen and Monica.

Also, to those whose assistance was acknowledged in
the first edition: Richard Callaghan, Museums Curator,
Redoubt Fortress, Eastbourne; Cav. Uff. J Keith Killby,
OBE, founder of the Monte San Martino Trust; Brian
Sims; and Mrs Elizabeth Comyn for permission to
include an excerpt from *Episodes* by Major John
Andrew Comyn, MBE.

The main records collections consulted were:

The United Kingdom National Archives:
Escape reports, interrogation questionnaires,
nominal lists and prisoner of war camp reports

The Imperial War Museum, London:
The Department of Documents

The United States National Archives
and Records Administration:
The Records of the Allied Screening Commission
(Italy)

*

The term 'British' was often used to cover British,
Commonwealth and Imperial forces.

To escape is generally to break free from confinement
in a prisoner of war camp or enemy country, and to
evade is to avoid or escape capture in enemy territory.

'Other ranks' indicates non-commissioned
officers and privates.

Partisans' aliases are shown in brackets
or inverted commas.

I have translated any items in Italian.

TIMELINE

1939

3 September: Great Britain, France, Australia and New Zealand declare war on Germany. Italy remains neutral.

1940

10 June: Italy declares war on Great Britain and France.

3-19 August: Italian forces occupy British Somaliland.

13 September: Italians advance into Egypt.

9 December: Successful British counter-offensive begins.

1941

January-May: Italy loses its East African Empire.

12 February: Rommel arrives in Libya as German forces join the war in North Africa.

11 December: Italy declares war on the United States.

1942

May-June: Axis (German and Italian) forces outflank the Gazala Line and take Tobruk.

23 October: Second Battle of El Alamein begins, leading to the eventual German and Italian retreat into Tunisia.

8 November: Allied invasion of Vichy French North Africa.

1943

12-13 May: Surrender of all Axis forces in North Africa.

10 July-17 August: Allied landings and conquest of Sicily.

24-25 July: Mussolini deposed and replaced by Marshal Badoglio. The war continues alongside the German ally.

3 September: Allied forces land in Calabria in southern Italy. The Italians sign terms of Armistice and Surrender with the Allies, which are made public five days later.

9 September: Allied landings at Salerno and Taranto. A Royalist Government is soon set up at Brindisi. The Germans occupy the rest of the country.

12 September: Mussolini rescued from the Gran Sasso by the Germans.

The Italian Social Republic is established at Salò.

13 October: Italian Royalist Government declares war on Germany and becomes a co-belligerent.

The Gustav (winter) line is created by the Germans.

1944

4 June: The Allies take Rome.

11 July: An awards bureau for Italian helpers, the Allied Screening Commission, is created.

4 August: 8th Army enters Florence.

The Allies advance beyond Massa in Tuscany and Rimini in the Romagna.

The Germans establish a new defensive position, the Gothic Line, and the front is largely static over the winter.

1945

April: The Allied offensive resumes in east and west.

2 May: German and Fascist forces surrender unconditionally after 20 months of war in Italy.

13 December: The administration of northern Italy is transferred to the Italian Government and the work of the Allied Military Government is complete.

1946

2 June: A constitutional referendum is held in Italy. As a result, the monarchy is replaced by a republican form of government.

1947

10 February: The Treaty of Peace with Italy is signed in Paris between Italy and the victorious powers of World War II, formally ending hostilities.

10 April: The Allied Screening Commission (Italy) closes its doors.

INTRODUCTION

I first came to write my military history books as the direct result of my family's experience of the Second World War.

In September 1943 the Allies landed in southern Italy. The Germans occupied the rest of the country and installed the deposed dictator, Benito Mussolini, as head of a puppet Fascist republic.

I had relatives on either side of the front line. My British father was a soldier with the advancing 8th Army, while my Italian mother and grandparents lived in the village of Castell'Arquato, province of Piacenza, within the Fascist north.

The local area was the scene of the greatest prisoner of war escape in Italy. At noon on 9 September over 500 British and Allied servicemen marched out of camp 49 Fontanellato, just before the arrival of a German column sent to capture them. Amongst the brave Italians who helped the escapers were my mother and grandparents. At the end of the war, they were awarded the 'Alexander Certificate' in recognition of the help they gave to 20 British and South African soldiers, which enabled them to escape or evade capture by the enemy.

My father, Quartermaster Sergeant Kenneth Winston Tudor, arrived in Piacenza with the liberating 8th Army in May 1945. He met my mother, Clara Dall'Arda, when she was working as translator for the Allied Military Governor. My parents were married in Swindon in 1948 and moved to my father's hometown of Newtown, Montgomeryshire, where I was born.

I grew up with stories of war and escape. The window shutters of my grandparents' house in Castell'Arquato were still peppered with bullet holes. On 5 April 1945 the partisans had routed an enemy force sent to blow up the river bridge. The fighting had spread into the garden.

I decided to find out more. I was able to meet some of the comrades of the escapers whom my family had sheltered and spent many hours of research in the British National Archives at Kew.

It was the logical next step to collate the precious information. And so in 2000 my first book, *British Prisoners of War in Italy: Paths to Freedom*, was born. It went on to sell hundreds of copies. I was pleased that amongst the earliest readers were many of the former prisoners of war in Italy, who immediately gave it their stamp of approval. This new, expanded and revised edition brings the story up to date, while retaining the popular elements from the original.

I am proud of my Anglo-Italian heritage. In my books I cover the life and times of some remarkable people. It is a pleasure to share this experience with readers from all over the world.

*

Winston Churchill, wartime prime minister from 10 May 1940 to 26 July 1945, wrote in his classic six-volume history, *The Second World War:*

In the weeks following the September armistice officers and men of the Italian Army stationed in German-occupied northern Italy and patriots from the towns and countryside began to form partisan units and to operate against the Germans and against their compatriots who still adhered to the *Duce*. Contacts were made with the Allied armies south of Rome and with the Badoglio Government. In these months the network of Italian resistance to the German occupation was created in a cruel atmosphere of civil strife, assassinations, and executions. The insurgent movement in central and northern Italy, here as elsewhere in occupied Europe, convulsed all classes of the people.

Not the least of their achievements was the succour and support given to our prisoners of war trapped by the armistice in camps in northern Italy. Out of about eighty thousand of these men, conspicuously clothed in battle dress, and in the main with little knowledge of the language or geography of the country, at least ten thousand, mostly helped by the local population with civilian clothes, were guided to safety, thanks to the risks taken by members of the Italian Resistance and the simple people of the countryside.

As a young war correspondent in South Africa in 1899, Winston Churchill had been captured during a Boer attack on an armoured train.

He reported: 'I left the State School's prison in Pretoria by climbing the wall when the sentries' backs were turned momentarily. I walked through the streets of the town without disguise, meeting many burghers, but was not challenged in the crowd.' Churchill jumped onto a goods train and hid under sacks of coal. He left the train next morning and eventually knocked on the door of John Howard, Manager of Transvaal Collieries, and asked for help.

The stranger replied: 'Thank God you have come here! It is the only house for 20 miles where you would not have been handed over. But we are all British here and we will see you through.' Churchill was hidden in a coal mine and then on a train carrying bales of wool. He was able to escape to Lourenço Marques in Portuguese Mozambique.

Winston Churchill's youthful experience as a successful escaper guided British policy towards the prisoners of war at large in Italy more than four decades later and informed his tribute to the Italians in his memoir.

This is the story of those wartime escapers and their local helpers, providing both an overview and a wealth of examples of the fascinating interaction between two diverse groups of foreigners, divided by war but united in humanity.

1

PATHS TO FREEDOM

In the late summer of 1943, thousands of men from many of the finest regiments and corps in the British Army arrived in the countryside of northern Italy as fugitives, hunted by Germans and Fascists alike. This is the story of some of those escaped prisoners of war and of the Italian civilians who helped them in Emilia-Romagna, including my mother and grandparents.

The servicemen were given sanctuary in the hills and valleys of the provinces of Parma and Piacenza. In this beautiful area to the west of the ancient Via Emilia, the Apennines rise suddenly from the plain, like cliffs on the shore of some shallow sea, which is what they were millions of years ago. Streams have cut almost parallel channels through the hill ridges, creating pretty tree-lined valleys. They are not dissimilar to those in parts of upland Britain.

The area has strong links to the United Kingdom through emigration. Italians had left their homes to find employment in large numbers since the early years of the twentieth century. London, Scotland and Wales were popular destinations. Many of the emigrants had done sufficiently well to be able to return to their homeland in the 1920s and 1930s, thus avoiding wartime internment.

My Italian grandparents came separately to London in the early years of the last century. They were from neighbouring small villages in the province of Piacenza. My grandfather, Alfredo Dall'Arda, found employment as a leading man in silent films and then became a waiter. He met a young confectioner called Giuseppina Volponi in London's thriving 'Little Italy' community and on 16 March 1914 they were married at Saint Peter's Italian Church in Clerkenwell.

Alfredo served in the Italian Army on the Austrian front during the First World War, returning to London once peace was restored. My mother, Clara Dall'Arda, was born on 29 August 1920 at the family home, 368, City Road.

Grandfather worked as a chef in several leading hotels in the capital, including the Ritz and the Savoy, and in 1928 opened his own restaurant at 4, Upper James Street, off Golden Square, W1. The business prospered and extended to the premises of the French restaurant next door. Male diners always received a large complimentary cigar, while ladies were given a fresh red rose.

Three years later, Alfredo took the family back to Italy. They settled in my grandmother's home village of Castell'Arquato, in the foothills of the Apennines.

My grandparents purchased a large villa with a nice garden, on Via Guglielmo Marconi, at the bottom of the village. Grandmother Giuseppina also inherited a share in a farm in the pretty vine-covered hills above Castell'Arquato. Life was good - until on 10 June 1940 Benito Mussolini took Italy into the Second World War on the German side.

*

When the escaped prisoners of war first arrived in the Apennines in September 1943, the barns were full and the grape harvest, *la vendemmia*, was a few weeks away.

Many of the farms were still run on the *mezzadria* system, which dated from medieval times. The landowner, or *padrone*, provided the farmhouse, outbuildings and implements, while a *mezzadro*, or sharecropper, worked the land with his family. The harvest and income were shared equally with the proprietor. The farmers encountered by escapers were frequently sharecroppers, with a landlord living in a nearby village or town.

The farms were largely self-sufficient in foodstuffs. Every patch of land was cultivated. The holdings produced grain, vegetables and wine. Pigs, rabbits, turkeys, chickens, guinea fowl and pigeons were kept for the table. A few cows lived indoors all year in stalls. Two large white oxen pulled the plough.

Wheat and wine were the main cash crops. The grain was taken to a mill and ground on giant stones powered by a water wheel, producing flour for bread and pasta and bran that was fed to the chickens. The grapes were trodden by foot. The juice was fermented and matured in oak barrels in the cellars, producing strong red wines such as *Gutturnio* and a sparkling white *Moscato*.

There was no electricity, mains water or telephones. Open fires and stoves for cooking used wood off the farms. Light came from oil lamps and candles. And water was drawn from deep wells.

Such was the farm my grandparents owned, called *Bertacca*, sadly no longer ours, but fondly remembered.

It stands amongst trees on top of one of the ridges above the village. The huddle of buildings was once a small hamlet. Some years ago, workmen found an old inn sign in some rubble. There was also a church, which was overseen by an itinerant priest. Now its high ceiling and fading frescoed walls shelter nothing more precious than new season's wine.

*

In wartime the usual way of moving around the countryside was on foot, even over long distances. The roads were unmetalled and built for horse and cart. The few petrol-driven vehicles that travelled along them often left clouds of grey-white dust in their wake.

Tracks across the mountains had been used as trade routes for thousands of years, carrying agricultural products between the coast and plain.

At the turn of the nineteenth century, my 3x great grandfather, Antonio Volponi, and his wife, Rosa Arata, followed the trail from Liguria to Castell'Arquato and decided to settle. One of the couple's sons, Giuseppe, married a Maria Bonvicini, the daughter of another family of merchants with origins in Liguria. The fourth of their five granddaughters, Giuseppina, was my grandmother.

In contrast, my grandfather's family were poor farm workers in the hamlet of Chiavenna Rocchetta, commune of Lugagnano. My great grandfather, Giovanni Dall'Arda, was murdered by persons unknown on his way home from market. His wife, Maria Solari, was left to bring up the family on her own.

It is perhaps no surprise that one of their children, my grandfather Alfredo, would leave home and try to make a new life in Great Britain, or that his success would bring him back to Italy some two decades later.

During the Second World War, merchants from Liguria brought olive oil over the mountain tracks. It was exchanged in the village for wheat. By this time, even necessities were only available on the black market or for barter, as a result of the Allied naval blockade. The daily bread ration was just 150 grams. Supplies of precious grain were hidden from the Germans and Fascists in the attics of houses.

For many of the escaped prisoners of war, those same country trails would become paths to freedom.

2

AFRICAN PRELUDE

The majority of the British and Allied prisoners of war (POWs) in Italy had been captured during the great tank battles in the North African desert between 1940 and 1943. The fighting covered an area from Morocco to Egypt, but most of the men were taken in 1942 in Cyrenaica, the eastern province of the Italian colony of Libya.

In July 1940 Benito Mussolini's troops made border incursions into Kenya and the Sudan. In August they overran British Somaliland. On 13 September the Italians invaded Egypt and advanced 60 miles to Sidi Barrani. The British counter-offensive, Operation Compass, began on 9 December. General Archibald Wavell's forces stormed 500 miles across Cyrenaica as far as El Agheila, destroying the Italian 10th Army and taking 130,000 prisoners.

In East Africa the British attack began on 19 January 1941. Most of the fighting was over by May. British Somaliland was liberated and the Italian Empire of Ethiopia, Eritrea and Italian Somaliland was lost forever.

Lieutenant General Erwin Rommel arrived in the Libyan port of Tripoli on 12 February to take charge of a joint

German-Italian army, which included the new *Afrika Korps*. Three British soldiers were captured in the first clash with the general's forces on 24 February.

The status of Rommel's command grew to that of a Panzer Army, but in constitutional terms it was subordinate to Marshal Ettore Bastico, Italian Commander-in-Chief, and to the High Command in Rome. Italians of the 20th Armoured Corps and the 10th and 21st Infantry Corps served throughout the North African campaign. Allied servicemen, even if captured by the Germans, were with few exceptions handed over to the Italians.

During a 27-month campaign, the motorised German-Italian Army twice battled its way 1,500 miles as far as western Egypt, but each time was forced to retreat. The speed and scale of these offensives led to the capture of large numbers of servicemen.

The second major attack was launched in 1942. According to Wavell's successor as Commander-in-Chief of the Middle East forces, General Claude Auchinleck: 'On 21 January the improbable occurred and without warning the Axis forces began to advance.'

Benghazi was taken and the 8th Army pushed back to lines between Gazala and an old fort at Bir Hacheim. On 26 May Rommel's troops swept south, engaging the main British armour at a crossroads nicknamed Knightsbridge and retaking Tobruk on 21 June.

Thirty-three thousand Allied troops were captured, including the entire South African 2nd Infantry Division. Rommel was promoted to Field Marshal. El Alamein was occupied on 30 June, the westernmost point reached by Axis forces in Egypt, only 80 miles from the important naval base of Alexandria. Panic set in at Cairo.

Former POW and the founder of the Monte San Martino Trust, Keith Killby, commented: 'Perhaps more than half of the POWs who were in Italy were captured in those battles.'

The first Battle of El Alamein in July 1942 was a stalemate. The 8th Army was victorious at the second in October and November.

On 8 November British and American forces invaded French North Africa - Morocco, Algeria and Tunisia - in Operation Torch. In response, the Germans occupied Vichy France and invaded Tunisia, while the Italians took over Corsica. Rommel's army also crossed into Tunisia from Libya in February 1943. Most of the United States' personnel held in Italy were captured during this campaign. The others were usually airmen.

After fierce fighting, all Axis forces in North Africa surrendered on 13 May 1943. The myth of the invincibility of Rommel and the *Afrika Korps* had been shattered and famous Italian divisions had been decimated - the *Ariete,* the *Bologna*, the *Brescia*, the *Folgore*, the *Littorio* and the *Pavia*.

Hundreds of thousands of Italians had been taken prisoner and sent to camps across Great Britain, the British Empire and the United States. Amongst them was our dear cousin, Lieutenant Germano Legati from Castell'Arquato, who ended the war as a prisoner of the British at a camp in India.

It is no surprise that many Italians came to believe that their days in the war were numbered, or that they would feel sympathy for the servicemen their own country held as prisoners of war.

*

Axis forces sought to evacuate captured personnel from forward areas as soon as possible. This was a requirement of international humanitarian law in the Geneva Convention relative to the Treatment of Prisoners of War (1929). It also reduced the problems in guarding and supplying such vast numbers of demoralised prisoners.

In the aftermath of battle, large transit camps were created along the coast at Derna, Benghazi, Barce, Tripoli and Tunis, or slightly inland as at Tarhuna. There was a great deal of improvisation, with tents often used to shelter the prisoners. At Derna, conditions were said to be primitive and chaotic. The staple diet was hard biscuit and tinned meat and even those were in short supply.

Problems of overcrowding were increased by the fall of Tobruk to Axis forces on 21 June 1942. Many of the captured Allied officers were flown to southern Italian airports such as Lecce in Puglia. Some went by submarine. 'Other ranks' were usually consigned to a variety of surface craft. Months later, many officers saw their men arriving in the camps from North Africa and were appalled by their emaciated condition.

The principal North African ports for Axis troop and supply convoys were Benghazi, Tripoli and later Tunis. The POWs were taken as human cargo on the return journey to Italy.

The single most important route was from Tripoli to Naples, which involved a basic journey of two or three days, though evasive action when leaving coastal waters often added several more to the voyage. The course lay along the coastline of Libya and Tunisia as far as Cape Bon and then at speed to Naples or the Sicilian ports of Trapani and Palermo. The route from Benghazi usually ran directly across the Mediterranean to Brindisi or sometimes Taranto. An alternative itinerary passed through Piraeus in Greece before landfall in Italy.

The prisoners were usually confined to the crowded holds of the Italian ships. The names of the vessels are seldom mentioned in their accounts, only the dire conditions and the ever present fear that they would fall victim to attack by their own side. Lieutenant Tony Davies of the Royal Artillery sailed from Tunis to Naples in a former coal-ship of around 2,000 tons, which was filthy, dark, damp and bitterly cold. The only food was a little ship's biscuit, moistened with water from a bucket that was occasionally lowered down.

Several of the prison ships were attacked by British submarines. This led to over 2,000 fatalities amongst Allied prisoners of war alone.

Brian Sims, the son of one of the lost servicemen, has established from official records that 42,719 captives were carried in 49 Italian ships over the year to December 1942. The British submarine Sahib P212 sank the Italian cargo steamer SS Scillin eight and a half miles off the Tunisian coast on 14 November 1942. She was following the course from Tripoli to Trapani and carrying 814 Allied POWs. Only 27 survived. The fatalities included Brian's father, Driver William Sims, Royal Army Service Corps, who was aged 30. The Italians provided the ship's embarkation roll to the British Ministry of Defence in 1944, but the reason for the loss of the prisoners was withheld from their relatives until the 1990s.

Five other prison ships had been attacked in the previous 11 months. The Ariosto was sunk by HMS P38 in February 1942, the Tembien later in the month by HMS Upholder P37, and the Loreto by HMS Unruffled P46 in October. The Sebastiano Venier was torpedoed by HMS Porpoise N14 and beached in December 1941. The Nino Bixio was hit by HMS Turbulent N98 in August 1942 and towed into port.

In April 1943 the Sahib was attacked by an Italian destroyer and German aircraft in the Straits of Messina and the crew were taken captive. They were imprisoned in Italy with the survivors of another submarine company. HMS Splendid P228 had been scuttled after attack by the German destroyer Hermes south east of Capri. The submariners were taken for interrogation to a camp in northern Germany, but afterwards were sent back to prison camp 52 Chiavari in Italy. Airmen and parachutists amongst Allied captives also received the attention of German military intelligence.

*

The first sight of their new home for most of the prisoners of war arriving from North Africa was the beautiful coastline of southern Italy or the Bay of Naples. The panorama of sea and sky is dominated by brooding volcanoes. Right on cue, they erupted during the Italian campaign.

3

CAPTIVES IN ITALY

After capture in North Africa, 80,000 Allied soldiers, sailors and airmen were held in Italy for an indeterminate period. The prisons, known as *campi di concentramento*, were spread across the peninsula. They varied a great deal from site to site. Some were purpose built on the barracks-style plan, which was designed to limit the chances of escape. A wide variety of buildings were also adapted for use, including schools and colleges, hotels and large villas, factories and monasteries.

After passing through the transit camps in the south of Italy (which sometimes took months) the prisoners were usually taken to more permanent prisons along the country's extensive network of railways. The larger camps were the size of small towns.

By September 1943 some of the Allied servicemen had been held captive for over three years. Flight Lieutenant Bill Rainford at camp 49 in Fontanellato, near Parma, was said to have been shot down in a Blenheim bomber over Bardia in north eastern Libya on 10 June 1940, the day Italy entered the war.

Camp reports and summaries, which can now be viewed at the British National Archives at Kew, show that the War Office possessed a reasonable amount of information on the location and strength of the main camps.

Italy was divided into five PM or *Posta Militare* (Military Post) districts, each with its own number: north western Italy, 3100; northern Italy, 3200; central Italy, 3300; the Naples area, 3400, and southern Italy, 3450. To identify the camps within each area, a PG or *Campo di Prigionieri di Guerra* (Prisoner of War Camp) number was used. The first was PG 5 in PM 3100, which was Gavi, 'Italy's Colditz.' The inmates had made at least one escape attempt from another camp and were officially described by the Italians as 'very dangerous.'

In December 1942 the Red Cross and Saint John War Organisation, the main voluntary body in Britain concerned with the welfare of prisoners, published a map and list of the camps for relatives of the detainees. Forty-two prisons were named, 12 with locations 'not known,'as well as 16 POW hospitals and 7 internment camps for civilians. The public were reminded to use the PM and camp number on letters or parcels sent to imprisoned servicemen, and not to add the geographical location.

The most comprehensive official list was compiled by the British War Office in August 1943. It gave details of 50 camps, 4 work camps and 18 hospitals. Fifty-two camp numbers were noted. Another six were 'not known.'

In the summer of 1942 work had been made compulsory for physically able privates and lance corporals on projects unrelated to the Italian war effort. Officers were not compelled to work, under the terms of the Geneva Convention.

Many sub-camps were set up to house the labour force. Some prisons in the north had over 20 satellites. Often they were many miles away from the base camp. As work requirements changed, the servicemen were frequently moved around Italy. Detachments provided casual labour on farms and vineyards, in factories and on building sites. The prisoners benefited from double rations, pay from a private employer and the chance to barter scarce goods with their guards and the civilians with whom they came into contact.

★

Naples, the main port for incoming prisoners from North Africa, had a large transit camp, PG 66 Capua, 16 miles to the north on the River Volturno. With over 6,000 prisoners in 5 compounds there were complaints of overcrowding, illness and the scarcity of Red Cross parcels. Just six miles away was PG 63 Aversa for Indian troops. In the mountains in the south of Campania was PG 35 Padula, housed in a famous monastery, the Certosa di San Lorenzo. There were also two hospitals for POWs, Caserta and PG 206 at Nocera.

Elsewhere in the south of Italy were PG 65 Gravina in Puglia, and in close proximity PG 51 Altamura and its military hospital, PG 204. Near the coast were two large transit camps, PG 85 at Tuturano, close to Brindisi, and PG 75 Bari, where conditions were especially harsh.

When Axis forces surrendered in North Africa in May 1943, it became clear that the invasion of the Italian mainland was likely. From June onwards, camps in the Naples area and southern Italy were closed. Most of the inmates were moved to prisons in central and northern Italy, though 1,771 were transferred to Germany.

By September 1943 the camps in PM districts 3400 and 3450 had all been evacuated. A few prisoners remained at hospitals and gaols or in isolated work detachments. The camps in the regions of Lazio and the Abruzzo were now closest to the front line.

Fourteen camps were in central Italy. Five miles south east of Rome was PG 122, near Cinecittà, the 'Italian Hollywood.' Twenty-five miles north east of the capital was PG 54 Fara-in-Sabina, with over 3,000 British and South African prisoners. Three other large camps were located in the Marche Region of eastern Italy: PG 53 Sforzacosta, near Macerata, PG 59 Servigliano, and PG 70 Monturano, near Fermo. To the south, over the border in the Abruzzo Region, was officers' camp PG 21 Chieti, situated near the Rome-Pescara road. Conditions were said to be bleak, with an administration dominated by Fascists. To the south west of Chieti were PG 78 Sulmona and PG 91 Avezzano, which was another camp for Indian troops.

In north western Italy, in addition to PG 5 Gavi, were PG 52 Chiavari, housed in barracks huts nine miles inland, and PG 106 Vercelli and PG 146 Mortara in the flat rice-growing area to the west of Milan, both with many associated sub-camps.

In the very large district designated PM 3200, northern Italy, there were 25 POW camps. PG 12 Vincigliata was a castle near Florence where British and South African higher ranks were held. They included generals Richard O'Connor and Philip Neame, the most senior British officers captured in North Africa. They were released on the Armistice and finally evacuated by sea in December after seven other rescue attempts had failed.

In Emilia-Romagna were officers' camps PG 19 Bologna and PG 47 Modena. Eleven miles to the north was PG 73 Carpi, where almost 5,000 'other ranks' included many captured at Gazala in June 1942. Their officers were later sent to PG 49 Fontanellato. Nearby was PG 55 Busseto. In the province of Piacenza was senior officers' camp PG 29 Veano, near Pontedellolio. Two other prisons in the Piacentine foothills, PG 41 Montalbo in the Valtidone, near Pianello, and PG 17 Rezzanello, in the Commune of Gazzola, were closed in the spring of 1943 and the inmates transferred to the new camp at Fontanellato.

In the north east of Italy were three large camps, each of which had many work detachments attached. PG 107 Torviscosa serviced the cellulose industry, PG 57 was at Grupignano, in the Udine area, and PG 103 near Ampezzo.

*

The 97 articles of the Geneva Convention of 1929 relative to the Treatment of Prisoners of War regulated the lives of the detainees in Italy, as elsewhere. The convention also gave the International Committee of the Red Cross (ICRC), the humanitarian agency with its headquarters in Geneva, a general mandate with respect to its application. On the basis of this article its delegates visited camps in Italy to monitor conditions and suggest improvements. Copies of their reports are also held at the British National Archives.

To further ensure the observance of the convention, a neutral state was appointed to represent British interests, known as the Protecting Power. Diplomats from the United States Embassy made inspections until their country entered the war on 11 December 1941. Then the Swiss took over and made most visits to the camps in Italy.

The neutral observers checked the organisation of the camps; food and clothing for the prisoners; hygiene; religious practice; mental and physical recreation; the prisoners' financial resources; prisoners' mail; the ways in which labour was employed; discipline and the conduct of any judicial proceedings against prisoners. The inspectors were able to interview detainees without the presence of Italian witnesses.

The Senior British Officer (SBO) in each camp was provided with an English copy of the convention.

Some categories of prisoners could be considered for repatriation and many detainees made representations to the inspectors. In the camps, a mixed medical commission considered claims based on serious physical or psychiatric illness, age or infirmity. Medical personnel were also eligible. In addition, there were claims by captured war correspondents that as non-combatants they too should be considered for repatriation.

One of the former POWs, Michael Ross, wrote of the routine at PG 35 Padula in his book, *From Liguria with Love*:

> The Geneva Convention laid down the rules which the Italians complied with scrupulously. Apart from being over-cautious on security matters, which we often found irksome, they did their best to make life as tolerable as possible.
>
> Orders from the Italian commandant were passed on to us through the Senior British Officer. As in any normal army unit, camp orders, containing instructions and general information, were posted up daily under the authority of the SBO. He appointed a small staff from among the prisoners to assist in the day to day running of the domestic affairs of the camp. Within the area of the monastery allotted for our own use, and to which we were strictly confined, we were virtually independent.

This stability was abruptly changed by the escape of 10 prisoners through a tunnel. They were recaptured. At first there were mild sanctions on the whole camp, but these were soon followed by the replacement of the Italian commandant with a less amenable *Carabiniere* (military police) *colonnello.* Captain Ross was an officer in the Welch Regiment. Later in the war he escaped to Monte Carlo and in 1946 married one of the twin daughters of an Italian family which had sheltered him.

In each camp an Escape Committee reported to the SBO and sanctioned the schemes thought most likely to succeed. In the words of one of the POWs, Michael Gilbert: 'You could tunnel under the walls, you could climb over the walls, or you could walk out of the gate.'

Many ex-prisoners comment on how adept the Italians were at keeping them behind bars. Only a handful of Allied servicemen made a home run before the Armistice of September 1943. Italian official figures suggest that between December 1940 and July 1943 just six men succeeded. Four of those were repatriated from the Vatican City State after a prisoner exchange with the Italians.

★

On 29 August 1940 the British Government had agreed to a request from the ICRC to allow it to send parcels of food, clothing and other necessities to the prisoners of war in Europe. They were prepared by volunteers in every county in Britain for the National Red Cross and Saint John War Organisation. The parcels were consigned in bulk to Lisbon. They went on specially chartered Red Cross ships to Marseilles and on to Geneva by train. Supplies for Italy were sent to Milan in sealed wagonloads, ready for onward transmission to the camps.

Every POW was supposed to be sent a 5-Kilogram food parcel four times a month, though its delivery was often disrupted through the vagaries of war. The parcels were a valuable addition to the basic Italian prison ration of bread, macaroni or rice, meat, cheese, tomato purée, peas and beans and coffee substitute.

A week after returning from Italy, Lieutenant Colonel Hugh Mainwaring, an escaper from PG 49 Fontanellato, told the *Montgomeryshire Express* of 30 October 1943 how grateful the prisoners of war were for the parcels of food and clothing supplied by the Red Cross. The lot of the men was vastly improved by those gifts.

The colonel said:

> I am particularly well. If we had not had those Red Cross parcels one could not have kept so well and would otherwise have found the job of escaping a very difficult one. If you are well then you can easily get about, but if you are not fit then it is 'a hell of a job' trekking about the country. It is the Red Cross parcel which makes all the difference.

Colonel Mainwaring, aged 37, a staff officer since 1940, played a prominent part in the desert campaign and was awarded the Distinguished Service Order (DSO). In November 1942 he was General Staff Officer (Grade 1) to General Montgomery, when he was captured during a forward reconnaissance.

Lieutenants Dan Billany and David Dowie, also prisoners at Fontanellato, wrote a novel entitled *The Cage*, which was based on real events. They lovingly listed the contents of a Red Cross food parcel. There was one tin each of biscuits, jam, meat and vegetables, margarine, carrots or tomatoes, meat roll, possibly bacon, cheese, and fish paste; two tins of sugar; two ounces of tea and four of chocolate; one tin of milk; a bar of soap; possibly raisins or porridge oats; sweets; pancake mixture and perhaps a tinned pudding.

★

The Central Agency of the ICRC at Geneva collated information on POWs. It was gleaned from lists provided by the Italians, the visits of its delegates to the camps and from the receipt of 'capture cards' sent in by the prisoners themselves. Details were provided to the British authorities, who would then advise the captives' anxious relatives. The Agency also forwarded messages to and from the prisoners. They were allowed to send two letters and four postcards a month without payment, though disruption of the mail was a common complaint made to the neutral camp inspectors.

The Vatican City State also played its part in transmitting news of prisoners of war by weekly English-language broadcasts on its radio and the carrying of prisoners' mail by couriers for distribution through neutral countries.

In 1941 Pope Pius XII appointed a Nuncio to minister to the spiritual and material needs of the prisoners. Emissaries from the Pope visited the camps at Christmastime in 1942 and gave each prisoner a Christmas carol and calendar booklet, which many of the ex-prisoners and their relatives still remember today.

A British-born private serving in the South African Army, Jack Rossiter of the 1st Royal Natal Carbineers, used his booklet to keep a daily diary when he escaped with two companions from a farm work camp controlled by PG 65 Gravina. In prison in Manfredonia in Puglia at the Armistice as guests of the 93rd Blackshirt Battalion, they escaped again and were liberated by British troops near Foggia on 28 September 1943. Jack Rossiter published his diary in Britain 49 years later.

★

In early September 1943 the Allies invaded the Italian mainland from Sicily, with landings at Reggio, Salerno and Taranto.

Eighty thousand of their countrymen were in the kingdom already as POWs. Official Allied figures detailed 79,533 captives. They were of diverse nationalities: 42,194 British; 26,126 from the empire; 9,903 European allies (Free French, Greeks, Russians and Yugoslavs) and 1,310 from the United States. Hundreds more would have been captured during continuing military operations. Most of the prisoners were soldiers and the majority of them had been captured in Libya in 1942. The rest were airmen from across the Mediterranean Theatre, ship and submarine crews, and some merchant seamen, often from convoys to Malta.

As the British 8th Army landed at Reggio di Calabria on 3 September, Italians in Sicily were about to sign an Instrument of Armistice and Surrender of their Armed Forces. Its third condition read:

> All prisoners or internees of the United Nations [the official name for the Allies] are to be immediately turned over to the Allied Commander-in-Chief and none of these may now or at any time be evacuated to Germany.

Senior British Officers in each prisoner of war camp were still under secret orders sent out in June to prevent mass breakouts of prisoners, so as to avoid the threat of reprisals. Italian camp commandants, on the other hand, were instructed by their war office during its last days to ensure that the Germans did not capture the prisoners, and to facilitate and assist their escape.

All these plans were quickly overtaken by events. When the terms of the Armistice were made public on 8 September, Germany attacked its former ally with great speed and ruthlessness. Rome was seized and the Italian King, Victor Emmanuel III, and his government forced to flee south to the Allies in Brindisi. Commanding officers in garrisons all over Italy tried in vain to contact their superiors in Rome to clarify the situation.

The public, already tired of a war imposed on them for reasons of imperial grandeur, found that it had been replaced by a new one, even more savage than the first. As well as two feuding foreign armies on its soil, Italy faced a bitter civil war between neo-Fascists and the emerging Resistance movement.

Amidst this chaos, the glittering prospect of freedom emerged for most of the prisoners of war in Italy.

4

THE PRISON CAMP

The unforeseen military and political upheavals in Italy during the summer of 1943 allowed the early release of thousands of British and Allied prisoners of war. The change in their fortunes is best documented in the case of those held in a famous prison camp in northern Italy.

Sixty-nine miles south of Milan, just off the Via Emilia, is the ancient village of Fontanellato, small, compact and peaceful around its moated castle, the Rocca Sanvitale. The commune is in the middle of the north Italian plain, where wheat and Indian Corn, sugar beet and tomatoes, vegetables and grapes, ripen early in large, open fields.

On the first of April 1943 a prison camp for Allied servicemen opened in a new building on the eastern edge of the village, just outside the historic centre. There was already a POW camp in the province of Parma, PG 55 at Busseto for 'other ranks,' only nine miles to the north west, as well as two internment camps for enemy civilians at Scipione and Montechiarugolo.

The first inmates of the new camp were transferred from the castles at Montalbo and Rezzanello in the adjoining province of Piacenza. Over the next few weeks they were joined by parties from prisons in central and southern Italy: PG 21 Chieti, PG 35 Padula, PG 66 Capua and PG 78 Sulmona.

The wartime camp was housed in the last of a trio of buildings created along the Viale IV Novembre by the Dominican Order of Preachers. First is the Sanctuary of the Blessed Virgin of the Sacred Rosary of Fontanellato, then the Convent of San Giuseppe, and finally the National Orphanage of the Madonna of Fontanellato. It was completed just prior to the outbreak of war, but instead of providing a home for little orphans it was surrounded by watchtowers and barbed wire and became PG 49, a detention centre for hundreds of Allied servicemen.

Some of the prisoners complained that their new billet was over-crowded. They found that there was a lack of privacy and no outside space in which to exercise. Even the pretentious building was actually very flimsy. But a more common sentiment was expressed by the Honourable Philip Kindersley, a Coldstream Guards captain, who later described it as 'the Ritz Hotel of prison camps.'

The Italians arranged for the closed order of nuns in the convent next door to provide the prisoners with a laundry and mending service. From time to time the men found notes with their clean washing saying that the sisters were praying to the Madonna on their behalf. The captives sent back little gifts of soap, tea and chocolates with messages of thanks.

Captain Leonardo Trippi, Attaché at the Swiss Legation in Rome, inspected the camp on 14 May 1943. He was already sympathetic to the Allies and was to become one of their helpers in the capital.

The captain reported that PG 49 was the best prison his team had visited in Italy. The lodgings and the interior arrangements were comfortable and the camp well organised.

The morale of the prisoners was high and they were on excellent terms with the Italian commandant, Lieutenant Colonel Eugenio Vicedomini. The SBO, Lieutenant Colonel DS Norman, had said that he was 'perfectly agreeable.'

There were already 540 prisoners in the camp: 502 soldiers, 10 sailors and 28 airmen. Four hundred and seventy-nine of the men were British, 57 came from other Commonwealth countries and 4 from the United States. Most of the captives were junior officers - captains, lieutenants and second lieutenants - in their twenties and thirties. There were also 114 'other ranks' who were paid ten shillings a month by the officers to act as orderlies: valets or attendants, often known as batmen.

The force guarding the prisoners consisted of around 70 Italian soldiers. Colonel Vicedomini had fought alongside British troops in the campaign against the Austrians in 1917. He had a good relationship with his Allied counterparts at PG 49. In turn, these were lieutenant colonels DS Norman, NE Tyndale-Biscoe and Hugo de Burgh. The Italian second-in-command was even friendlier to the captives. Captain Mario Jack Camino was smart and charming. He had an English wife and mother and had been in business in Slough before the war. The captain shared the role of interpreter with Lieutenant Peredini. In peacetime he was a Thomas Cook representative, but was now treated with some suspicion by the prisoners as the Security Officer. There were four other officers, a sergeant major and about 60 guards.

The report reveals that the total camp area covered 210,000 square feet. Ninety-two thousand were covered with structures. The rest was open and could be adapted for sports grounds. The captives were interned in a four-storey house, solidly built of stone and brick. Offices, mess rooms and showers were located on the ground floor. Officers' dormitories, a high and vast hall, a bar, recreation rooms and a barber's shop occupied the next level. There were more officers' dormitories on the third floor, while the top level was given over to the 'other ranks.'

The dormitories were high and airy. Large windows let in plenty of sun and air and overlooked the fertile plain. The rooms had electric lights and central heating. The officers had the luxury of iron beds with elastic springs, mattresses of wool, horsehair or artificial fibre, and bed linen and two blankets. There were bedside cabinets, a wardrobe for every two officers, and tables and chairs. The biggest dormitory accommodated 30 men. The SBO had a large room to himself.

The 'other ranks' had three rooms, which were well ventilated and adequately lit. Fifty-three orderlies shared a large dormitory and another 61 were in two inter-connected rooms. They slept in double-tier wooden beds, with a mattress and two blankets each. The men also had a large corridor with tables and chairs at their disposal.

Captain Trippi remarked that the house looked very clean. As it was spacious and the rooms large, keeping the marble staircases and tiled floors tidy involved a great deal of effort. Colonel Norman complained that the orderlies had too much work to do, as there was only one for every four officers.

The colonel told Captain Trippi that the kitchen was ably managed and the food well cooked and abundant. The catering was directed by Lieutenant Leon Blanchaert, a Belgian on the British Army's General List.

There were separate kitchens for the officers and men on the ground floor. The stoves were lit at 5.30 in the morning, the kettles put on the wood-burning ranges, and the fires maintained all day. The prisoners ate in two nicely arranged mess rooms in the basement. In their own canteens they could also purchase food items that were not rationed. The officers received tickets to buy a glass of vermouth and one of red wine a day. A free tobacco allowance was issued.

A stock of about 3,000 Red Cross parcels was on hand at the time of the inspection. They were not passed to individuals, as in many camps, but placed in a central store. Captain CD (Kit) Patterson of the Royal Northumberland Fusiliers was in charge of the distribution of food and supplies. Personal items such as soap, chocolate and cigarettes were issued to the prisoners once a week. The daily food requirements were delivered to the kitchens to supplement the Italian rations. The local allowance for officers was identical to that of the civilian population, while the batmen received the enhanced amount given to workmen.

The prisoners also had access to items on the black market. They used cigarettes and other surplus items from Red Cross parcels to bribe their guards into obtaining food from local farmers, including Parma ham and Parmesan cheese.

To pay for food and sundry expenses, the captives received regular amounts in camp currency. By a private arrangement between the governments, the servicemen were entitled to the same wage as Italians of the corresponding rank. Craftsmen such as tailors, cobblers and barbers received an extra three lire and sixty cents a day.

Once the Swiss observers had inspected the camp, they sat down in an office with Colonel Norman to discuss the prisoners' welfare. The colonel had an English copy of the Geneva Convention and no Italians were present. Any men with requests or claims were called in. No complaints were made to the inspectors regarding the camp. This reflects the fact that it adequately catered for all the essentials of POW life.

There was a small infirmary with rooms for officers and men. An Italian surgeon superintended the service, with three medical officers and an attendant from amongst the prisoners at his command. The clinic was well provided with medicines and had 900 comfort and invalid parcels at the time of the inspection. In an adjacent room, South African dentist Captain Marcus Kane-Burman had set up a busy surgery with instruments provided by the Italians.

The camp had a small Roman Catholic chapel and rooms set aside for Protestant observance. There were two chaplains, a Presbyterian and a member of the Church of England.

The prisoners could stay outdoors from eight in the morning to seven in the evening in the courtyard, a cobbled area about 20 yards wide at the rear of the orphanage. Captain Trippi noted that a large area could also be used for recreation, but that it needed levelling. The commandant was obtaining the necessary material. The prisoners also had the opportunity to go on walks under guard.

There was a gallery above the hall, furnished with tables and chairs, where the inmates could play cards, chess and ping-pong. A library room contained about 3,000 books and it was open for an hour in the morning and at noon.

*

Work on creating a playing field gave the prisoners the opportunity to excavate a hiding place and to make the only successful escape before the Armistice.

Captain Michael Ross and Lieutenant Jimmy Day left the field after dark on 7 May and walked cross-country. They were arrested nine days later in Como by a suspicious *Carabiniere*.

The trench lay undiscovered and three captains escaped and travelled by train towards Milan on 9 May: Tony Roncoroni, Dominick (Toby) Graham and Peter Joscelyne. The trio were captured next morning and returned to the camp. Ross and Day joined them a week later. There was no punishment cell (or cooler) at Fontanellato, only a comfortable room on the ground floor with six spring beds. The escapers cheerfully served out the 30 days confinement imposed by Colonel Vicedomini.

The Italians completed the playing field and it reopened on 24 May. Restrictions on its use were imposed, leading to complaints by the SBO. However, the War Office sent a message to desist from more protests for the time being. They did not want the replacement of the Italian commandant by one less friendly to the Allied prisoners, as had happened at Padula.

Further escape attempts from PG 49 were difficult, as the camp was based on a single building. The basement was searched every day. A tunnel excavated by the Guards was discovered within a week. In response, the Italians dug a 10-foot trench around the camp, just above the level of the water table. At the end of June a project was launched to create a hiding place within the orphanage where men could scuttle if the Germans took over, but it was overtaken by events and never completed.

Lieutenant John (Jack) Andrew Comyn made one of the last attempts to escape from the camp. Twice a week he assisted an Italian Quartermaster Sergeant (QMS) in a store on the road just outside the wire. It housed items of clothing confiscated from parcels for fear that they could be used during escape attempts. The lieutenant was required to issue receipts in English. He managed to have his friend, Major Hugh Hope, appointed as his assistant.

On the chosen day, during the afternoon nap, or *siesta*, the major distracted the QMS while Comyn donned some of the clothing in the other room. He put on a workman's hat made of paper, rubbed himself with dust, picked up a hammer and jumped through an unlocked window.

There seemed to be nobody about. Jack Comyn walked along the road, past the wire and sentry boxes, and turned the left-hand corner of the camp in the direction of the village. He recalled:

> Suddenly a man in uniform stepped from behind a tree in front of me. I knew him well, he was the *Brigadiere* (a rank roughly equivalent to sergeant) of the *Carabiniere* detachment which supplemented the camp guards. *'Dove andate?'* [Where are you going?] he addressed me. Alas, my Italian was not good enough to maintain any pretence of being a building worker, certainly in face of a member of the *Carabinieri Reali*, one of the best police forces in Europe.
>
> Within a few minutes I was ushered into the office of the Camp Commandant. This was *Colonnello* Vicedomini, an elderly officer recalled from retirement. He was of the old school, a perfect gentleman, liked by all. The *Brigadiere* told him that I was *Tenente* Comyn, caught while trying to escape. I was still in my disguise, and at first the colonel refused to believe that it was me. When convinced, his consternation was amazing. 'But *Tenente* Comyn,' he exclaimed, 'my sentries on the wire might have shot you - and then what would your mother have said?' As I had not expected this question I was uncertain how to reply, but his concern touched me and I received with equanimity the statutory sentence of 28 days solitary confinement which he awarded.

*

The daily routine at PG 49 was similar to other camps. Roll call would be held in the courtyard at nine in the morning. The prisoners filed past two Italian officers to be counted.

This was followed by a breakfast of tea and biscuits or porridge on Sundays. The morning was spent attending classes or playing outdoor games.

After lunch, many men took a *siesta*. In the late afternoon there was the chance for further organised activities. A second roll call would be held at six in the evening. Dinner began at seven. Later, the bar run by 11th Hussars lieutenant Tommy Pitman and his team was open in the gallery.

Lectures were given in the camp on subjects as varied as agriculture, law, journalism and languages. Sports and entertainments were coordinated by Flying Officer Rainford. Football and rugby were especially popular. Athletic contests and boxing matches were organised and even races using boats made of wine corks that bobbed along a stream. Two bookmaking firms and regular football pools emerged to cater for the betting fraternity. The Flying Officer also ran a popular enterprise known as Opportunities Limited or 'Ops.' It offered an attractive range of goods and services and was officially designated the only means of sale and exchange.

Many prisoners played bridge and backgammon in the assembly hall or baccarat after dinner in the mess. It was possible to hire a piano and buy musical instruments, and several groups were formed to provide music for concerts and stage shows. There was a dramatics group and an artists' circle that organised a fine exhibition. There were plenty of volunteers to sit for portraits, while landscapes were inspired by views from the top floors of the orphanage across the plain towards the mountains. On clear days the panorama even extended to snow-covered Alps far to the north.

The walks were held before breakfast along quiet country lanes. The men were on parole, having promised not to escape, but they were still heavily guarded. David Dowie remembered women walking in the fields, the farm smells and children who ran to the gate to watch them pass. As well as giving the prisoners their only contact with the outside world, the excursions also provided them with a precise knowledge of the area around the orphanage, which would soon prove very useful.

The presence of a large POW camp was a major talking point in the village, which had a population of about 3,000. Younger residents were desperate to see the prisoners and soon found that they could wave to them from a tree-lined road that runs past the right hand side of the building and gives access to the cemetery.

David Dowie recalled:

> On Sunday, all the little girls from the village and all the smart, silk-stockinged evacuees from Parma make bright patches of colour on the dusty road. Flowers in hand to visit the cemetery; wind blown skirts; 40 yards and two rows of barbed wire and every window on that side of the building frames two heads, and each head two overworked eyes.

In contrast, prisoners who looked out of the windows at the front of the orphanage risked being fired upon by the guards in the watchtowers.

*

As the months of 1943 slipped by, Italy's days in the war seemed numbered. David Dowie related:

> Our sense of isolation as a community was progressively destroyed at Fontanellato by the news of the progress of the war. The offensive in North

Africa began again and, in May, Tunis and Bizerta fell.
North Africa, where we had nearly all been captured
in what seemed an endless scuffle, was now entirely
British. Barce, Derna, Benghazi, all these Axis bases
where we had languished as prisoners were now full
of British troops. The power of Britain had stepped
decisively towards us and freedom became a thing
to bear in mind.

In addition to the surrender of Axis forces in North Africa
in May, the Italians and Germans suffered major reverses in
Russia. At the same time, Allied aircraft swept across the plain
on bombing raids to the great northern Italian cities and
further into occupied Europe.

The Allied landings in Sicily on 10 July were followed
by a palace coup in Rome a fortnight later. On Monday,
26 July the three inch headline in the *Corriere della Sera*
newspaper read: 'The dismissal of Mussolini – Badoglio head
of the Government – His Majesty the King assumes command
of the Armed Forces.'

The news arrived at PG 49 in a radio broadcast relayed over
a loud speaker above the Italian orderly room. It was overheard
by a group of prisoners who were about to leave on a walk.

Dan Billany recalled that Captain Camino 'walked from
the hut smiling a quiet little smile – he spread his hands and
shrugged a little as he passed the Italian Orderly Officer, who
in turn raised his eyebrows. That was how they mourned the
Duce.' Other prisoners related that the guards poured into
the courtyard at the rear of the building, singing and dancing
with joy. Portraits of Mussolini were pulled from the walls and
stamped underfoot. Fascist symbols across the countryside were
removed or defaced. The Italians thought the announcement
of the fall of the dictator meant the end of the war for them.

One of two war correspondents in the camp, the American Larry Allen of the Associated Press, prepared news bulletins based on information gleaned from Italian newspapers and a secret radio in the camp. Every bulletin began with the word Flash. He reported Mussolini's removal with:'Flash, Benito *finito!*'

The Fascist party was outlawed and political prisoners released, but martial law was declared, an eight o'clock curfew imposed and meetings and assemblies banned.

Though the war continued, the new government began secret peace negotiations with the Allies at the beginning of August. A German request to send prisoners of war to Germany was rejected by Raffaele Guariglia, the new Italian foreign minister. In the meantime, extra German divisions poured over the Brenner Pass, Allied bombing raids continued and food riots broke out in the cities.

At Fontanellato the guards no longer fired at prisoners when they appeared in windows at the front of the building, but the walks were cancelled. It was feared that a friendlier populace might create security problems.

Lieutenant Colonel Hugo Graham de Burgh also arrived from Lucca Military Hospital (PG 202) in August and became the SBO. Aged 49, he was a member of an upper class Anglo-Irish family and veteran of the First World War, where he was Mentioned in Despatches and awarded the Military Cross (MC) for gallantry in action. The colonel was appointed OBE in 1921. He had been SBO at three camps before coming to PG 49. While at Lucca the officer had heard rumours of prisoners of war being sent to Germany.

Hugo de Burgh found the captives at Fontanellato demoralised. He asserted command and arranged for them to learn new skills and prepare themselves physically for escape.

Meanwhile, a new structure was superimposed upon the dormitory organisation. Five companies were created, four for officers and one for 'other ranks.' Each unit was composed of around a hundred men, with its own commander, adjutant, platoons, sections and an infantry capability. There were drills, daily situation reports and duty rosters. The men were ordered to smarten up their appearance.

The prisoners began to lay bets on the date when they would be able to walk out of the camp gates as free men. Hopes spiralled on 17 August when the Italians announced that Sicily had fallen. They seemed completely calm and resigned to the idea that the war had been lost.

A few days later, the captives cheered as a mighty armada of planes overflew the camp. They were identified as American B-17 Flying Fortresses. Based in Britain, they were returning from bombing the ball-bearing factory at Regensburg in Germany and were now making for Algiers. One of the aircraft was seen to be losing height and fire began to pour from its engines. A parachute drifted down and the Flying Fortress disappeared behind trees and exploded. The only survivor was picked up in the camp truck and brought to the Italian offices. He was soon driven away for interrogation, but not before the prisoners had sent him a Red Cross parcel, the quickest delivery ever recorded.

Lieutenant John Langrishe of the Royal Artillery (RA), a 28-year-old Cambridge law graduate, recalled:

> Further sensations came hot on the heels of one another. Now the Allies were ashore near Reggio di Calabria. Behind our barbed wire we began to envisage freedom within a matter of days. One small worry, however, clouded our otherwise encouraging outlook: how would the German Army react?

A large unit of their troops had already marched past the camp, singing loudly to intimidate the inmates.

Before dawn on 3 September the British 8th Army had crossed the Straits of Messina to invade the mainland. Later in the day, the Instrument of Armistice and Surrender of the Italian Forces was signed in Sicily. As we have seen, the third of 12 military terms said: 'All prisoners or internees of the United Nations are to be immediately turned over to the Allied Commander-in-Chief and none of these may now or at any time be evacuated to Germany.' The surrender remained secret for five days.

On 6 September the Italian War Office sent an order to its camp commandants:

> British POWs – Prevent them falling into German hands. In the event that it is not possible to defend efficiently all the camps, set at liberty all the white prisoners but keep the blacks in prison. Facilitate their escape either to Switzerland or along the Adriatic coast to southern Italy … The freed prisoners should be given reserve rations and directions as to which route they should follow.

Colonel de Burgh recalled that Colonel Vicedomini informed him that he had heard that prisoners were to be removed to Germany. The SBO asked what he intended to do and if he would give them some warning.

The commandant replied: 'I will. If you organise inside the wire, I will have cycle patrols out to bring information of any approach of German troops.'

Two days later, on the balmy evening of Wednesday, 8 September, the prisoners were relaxing after supper. Suddenly, a chaotic din was heard coming from the village.

At 7.43 in the evening, music on Italian radio had been interrupted by a broadcast from Marshal Badoglio.

He announced that the Italian Government had asked General Eisenhower for an armistice. The request had been accepted. Hostile acts towards Anglo-American forces on the part of the Italians would cease everywhere. However, they would respond to attack from any other quarter.

The prisoners ran to the windows of the orphanage and were amazed to see a large crowd come rushing down the road on cycles and on foot. The people shouted, sang and cheered and threw their hats in the air. 'Peace! Peace!' they cried. The guards flung down their rifles, stamped on them and hollered that the prisoners were now their friends.

The captives felt numb. What did it all mean? Their excited chatter was interrupted by an order that flashed around the building in a minute. The SBO would address all ranks in the main hall immediately.

Colonel de Burgh said:

> I have been informed by the commandant that the Italian Government has asked for an armistice. Beyond that I know nothing, but he has promised to keep me in immediate touch with the situation. In the meantime, it is absolutely essential that everyone keeps perfectly calm and behaves like a British officer.

The prisoners were forbidden from looking out of the windows, contacting civilians or leaving the building. There would be a parade in the courtyard at nine in the morning, when the colonel would give further details of the situation.

At the time there were 536 prisoners in the camp, made up of 483 officers and 53 men. Four hundred and twenty-nine of the captives were British Army personnel, including 27-year-old Londoner Ronald Noble, war correspondent from the Universal Press; 39 South African Army; 27 Indian Army;

2 New Zealand Army; 1 Canadian Army; 20 Royal Air Force; 17 Royal Navy; and the American war correspondent Larry Allen.

The men went to bed in a state of nervous excitement. Lookouts were posted in top floor rooms. What would the morning bring?

5

THE ESCAPE

The prisoners of war rose early in the camp at Fontanellato on 9 September after receiving news the evening before of the Armistice. At nine in the morning the SBO, Colonel de Burgh, addressed his men on the parade ground. He revealed that some time ago he had received instructions on such an eventuality from the War Office.

This was the notorious 'stand fast' order sent by the British escape and evasion secret service, MI 9, to the camps across Italy in June 1943. It read:

> In the event of an Allied invasion of Italy, Officers Commanding prison camps will ensure that prisoners of war remain within camp. Authority is granted to all Officers Commanding to take necessary disciplinary action to prevent individual prisoners of war attempting to rejoin their own units.

However, Colonel de Burgh said that he now believed that the instruction was out of date and did not reflect the situation on the ground.

Colonel Vicedomini had received information that there had been fighting since dawn in Parma and Piacenza between German and Italian troops. It was likely that the enemy would arrive at any moment to take over the camp.

A place was being found in the countryside where the prisoners could be hidden. The commandant had scouts on all the access roads to give early warning of any move on the camp.

The alarm signal would be three Gs blown on a bugle. If it were sounded, the prisoners were to assemble quickly in their companies. They would march out of the camp through a large gap in the wire, which would be cut by the Italians at the top end of the playing field. The men were to don battledress, collect a day's rations and be ready to evacuate the orphanage at five minutes notice.

The commandant issued the prisoners with small amounts of lire. The men cleared their rooms and chatted in the courtyard over a mid-morning cup of cocoa. Two German JU88 bombers suddenly roared over the camp. The captives scattered and dived to the ground, but the planes disappeared over the horizon without taking any hostile action.

The bar was busier than usual. In the kitchen, Lieutenant Blanchaert and his team began to prepare a special luncheon of cold salmon and new potatoes.

One British officer was already outside the wire. Colonel de Burgh had appointed Hugh Mainwaring his Chief of Staff and given him responsibility for coordinating the response to any emergency.

At 7.30 in the morning the commandant called on Colonel Mainwaring. He told him that the situation had deteriorated. The hiding place must be found urgently. The Italian gave the colonel a map of the area, suggested the best direction to take and said that Captain Camino would act as his guide.

The officers found a sanctuary five miles north west of the camp. The winding bed of the Rovacchia torrent - a tributary of the Taro - has steep banks covered with scrub, beeches and poplars.

As the pair arrived back at the camp, a patrol returned with the news that a German column had been sighted only two miles away. It was drawn up on the main road and ready to take over the camp.

An Italian bugler blew the pre-arranged alarm signal of three Gs. It was noon. The men sprinted from the orphanage into the courtyard. It would be the last time that they would parade in their five companies.

Led by Colonel Mainwaring and Captain Camino, the servicemen marched out in threes through the gap in the wire. A few Italians joined the column. Colonel Vicedomini and 40 of his men chose to remain. The march out was done quietly and in good order. By 12.10 the camp was empty of prisoners.

The walk to the hiding place took two hours. The country lanes were sweltering in the afternoon sun. But no one seemed to mind. They were so happy. Toby Graham recalled: 'One moment we were prisoners behind wire - the next, free men walking through sunlit vineyards, plucking at the near ripe grapes.'

The only incident was the appearance of another German aircraft. A Junkers 52 swooped over the column, so low that the crew could not but have noticed the prisoners' khaki uniforms with large red diamonds sown on the back.

The escapers spread out along the watercourse according to the areas chosen for each company by Colonel Mainwaring. They were ordered to stay together and take shelter in the surrounding trees, vineyards and fields of Indian Corn. If rescue were at hand, the men could return to the camp. If not, they were in a good position to disperse.

A steady trickle of Italians began to come across the fields. They brought supplies from Red Cross parcels and news of what had happened at the camp.

A couple of hours after the prisoners had fled, about 30 German infantrymen had arrived in lorries and two armoured cars. The soldiers fired shots over the heads of villagers who were carrying off supplies from the camp and stores. Two days later the Germans announced that looting would be treated as a capital offence. But for the orphanage it was too late. Everything moveable had gone.

On the morning of the escape, Dario Fava of the 3rd *Bersaglieri* Regiment, a native of Fontanellato, arrived with orders from Milan for Colonel Vicedomini, who was in the same infantry regiment.

Dario Fava recalled:

> So, at 10.30 or 10.45, I think, the order arrived to set the British free … When the Germans came they glimpsed the colonel. An SS lieutenant, accompanied by Pietralunga the interpreter, approached him and said:
>
> 'Where are the prisoners?'
>
> 'I had the order to liberate them,' replied Vicedomini.
>
> He barely had time to say this when the German lieutenant struck him savagely. Then he took away the pistol in the colonel's bandoleer and ordered his men to disarm all the guards. Then they made us go to the command centre and stack our weapons there.

The Germans dined on the cold salmon and new potatoes prepared for the prisoners, drank a lot of wine and vandalised as much of the camp as they could. Finally, after loading their trucks with booty, the soldiers drove off. Then the villagers returned.

Colonel Vicedomini was taken away by the Germans, together with his remaining officers, and sent to a POW camp in Poland. At the end of the war he returned to Italy in broken health and died soon afterwards. Colonel de Burgh described the commandant as being 'extremely kind and helpful during our meetings,' adding, 'he organised our escape and our shelter.'

The escapers spent a warm night under the stars. Heavy motorised transport could be heard on the main road. Its direction was unknown. Mysterious flashes lit the distant horizon.

Shortly after dawn, a procession of farmers and villagers began arriving with clothing, money and supplies. All the Italians knew where the prisoners were, but no one betrayed them to the Germans.

In the morning, Jack Comyn recalled:

> Colonel de Burgh and Hugh Mainwaring had anxious consultations, in which I took part because Hugh had enlisted me as a kind of staff officer, together with Leon Blanchaert. The SBO considered that he had obeyed the War Office orders, in that he had so far kept us all together. But it was clearly impossible to continue feeding 500 of us in the ravine, and the Germans might at any moment discover where we were.

Colonel de Burgh held a conference at one in the afternoon. He said that in view of the danger, the companies would leave the Rovacchia. They would move west and stand down. The dispersal would take place over the next two nights.

The servicemen could attempt to cross the Swiss border, or to join friendly forces in the south, though they were over

600 miles away. It was every man for himself. By evening, 200 men had been found billets on local farms.

Captain Camino guided Colonel de Burgh and his two staff officers, Lieutenant Colonel Richard Wheeler and Captain Reggie Phillips, to his home area of the Aosta Valley. Colonel Wheeler went off on his own, as it was thought that a party of three might be too conspicuous.

After four days of hard and dangerous climbing, Colonel de Burgh and Captain Phillips followed smugglers' trails to reach Zermatt in Switzerland on 29 September. They soon heard that Colonel Wheeler had also been successful in crossing the border.

In October 1945 Colonel de Burgh became head of the Allied Screening Commission, which had been set up to recognise and compensate persons who had assisted Allied personnel behind enemy lines after the 1943 Armistice.

Lieutenant Colonel Hugh Mainwaring was one of the earliest to leave the encampment. He was accompanied by Lieutenant Blanchaert and Greek lieutenant George Lascaris, both Italian speakers. Jack Comyn was asked to go with them, but reluctantly decided to stay with his regimental colleagues. 'It was,' he said later, 'one of the worst mistakes I ever made.'

The trio pretended to be Italian soldiers walking south to reach their homes. They were readily given permission to sleep in stables and haylofts and to gather fruit and vegetables from the fields. On 13 October the officers crossed British lines at Casacalenda, north west of Foggia. Like many other former POWs, Leon Blanchaert joined the Special Operations Executive (SOE) in Italy. In 1944 he was awarded the DSO.

At first most of the prisoners stayed on the plain near the camp. On 20 September the Germans began to raid local farms where escapers were known to be in hiding. Several were recaptured and their helpers arrested. Andrea Baruffini

PG. 54 FARA-IN-SABINA NORTH EAST *

OF THE CAPITAL. (25 MILES) *

PRISONERS ARRIVED JULY 1942 (3,000)

FOLLOWED BY 1900 MEN FROM 27/28
SEPTEMBER FROM PG 66 (TRANSIT CAMP)

AT CUPUA.

GUARDS DESERTED AT ARMISTICE
                    SEPT 1943

APENNINE MOUNTAINS,

APRIL '42 CAPTURED IN DESERT

APENNINE'S

ITINERANT

MOST MEN TAKEN. IN 1942 IN CYRENAICA
THE EASTERN PROVINCE OF THE ITALIAN
COLONEY OF LIBYA

21ST JAN 1942. BENGAHAZI TAKEN.

BY JUNE GERMANS HAD RETAKEN TOBRUK.
33K ALLIED PRISONERS TAKEN. OVER HALF
OF P.O.W^{s} TAKEN IN THIS BATTLE.
SURRENDER ON MAY 13TH 1943.

SO FAR AWAY (DBY ME)
  DIRE STRAIGHTS.

of Cannètolo, near the Torrente Rovacchia, was sent to the concentration camp at Mauthausen in Austria and never returned. At Fossoli prison before deportation he had left a note for his sons, Fortunato and Sandro, saying: 'Pray for me, destination unknown.'

Lieutenant John Langrishe helped with odd jobs on two farms near the camp, but on 29 September was forced to flee into the fields when a German sweep began. He left the area next day, together with Captain David Buchanan and Lieutenant John Eadie, both also from the Royal Artillery, and Lieutenant VA (Bunny) Buist of the Royal Armoured Corps. Scrambling over wire fences along the railway line, the escapers waited for gaps in German military traffic before crossing the busy Via Emilia. By evening they had walked 10 miles over the plain and into the foothills of the Apennines. Their first overnight stop was the large farm of Alberto Sanini at Vigoleno in the Stirone Valley. The men were made welcome and fed generously. The next night was spent in the hamlet of La Trinità.

Over the next two days the quartet crossed rough country to Pieve, south east of Bardi. Agostino Ferrari, a former chef at the Connaught Rooms in London, arranged shelter for the officers with different families over a period of two weeks. There were said to be two to three hundred ex-prisoners in the area. Most had decided to wait and see before hazarding the long journey to reach friendly forces or to cross the border to Switzerland.

The four officers decided to split into pairs. This was the best number for mutual support, while less likely to attract attention or overburden local resources. Lieutenants Eadie and Buist left for Tuscany, as they had heard that the cooking was the best in Italy. They did reach the region, but were recaptured and sent to prison camps in Germany.

Captain Buchanan and Lieutenant Langrishe also eventually parted on grounds of prudence at Fano in the Abruzzo after 42 days and 400 miles. The captain remained in the area and was liberated when it was overrun by Allied forces in 1944.

John Langrishe walked another 130 miles and led a hazardous crossing of German lines to American troops in the village of Cerro on 19 November. He received a Mention in Despatches for his actions. The lieutenant had always asked his hosts for a suggested route for the next day's journey and never wrote their names down in case of recapture.

John Langrishe's long walk out from Fontanellato to the Sangro took 7 weeks and a day in 34 stages. He returned to Great Britain and reached his front door in Edinburgh two nights before Christmas 1943.

*

When the Germans launched their raid on PG 49 on Thursday, 9 September they also targeted a nearby 'other ranks' camp. There were about 500 prisoners in PG 55 Busseto and its agricultural work camps. Only 10 to 15 men were able to escape from the main camp, housed in the Villa Pallavicino on the plain north west of Fontanellato. The villa is now the National Museum of Giuseppe Verdi.

Captives in three sub-camps succeeded in escaping, while another was taken over by the Germans. The satellite camps were across the River Po in the direction of Cremona. One hundred and fifty men escaped and some of them were the first to cross into Switzerland. In these early days the escape routes were still open and rail traffic was not subject to adequate security controls.

Soldier E Roberts recalled his experience at PG 55:

1. Harold Alexander, Allied commander.

2. British troops in North Africa, 1942.

3. SS Scillin, prison ship for Allied prisoners of war.

4. HMS Sahib P212, which sank the Scillin.

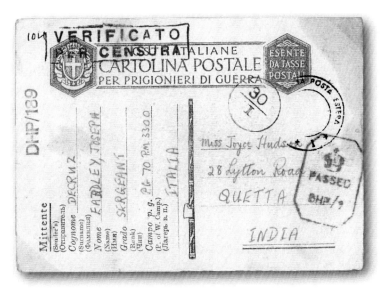

5. Prisoner of war postcard from camp 70 Monturano to India.

6. Currency at camp 73 Carpi.

7. In the grounds of the former camp 49 Fontanellato.

8. First steps to freedom – into the plain.

9. The Stirone Valley: escape route for escapers.

10. The Arda Valley: sanctuary for many POWs.

11. The village of La Trinita.

12. The escapers' hideout.

13. My mother and father, Castell'Arquato.

14. A German soldier checks documents near Milan.

This certificate is awarded to

Dall'Arda Alfredo fu Giovanni

as a token of gratitude for and

appreciation of the help given to the

Sailors, Soldiers and Airmen of the

British Commonwealth of Nations,

which enabled them to escape from, or

evade capture by the enemy.

H.R. Alexander

Field-Marshal,
Supreme Allied Commander,
1939-1945   *Mediterranean Theatre*

15. The 'Alexander Certificate' awarded to my grandfather.

I was working on a farm for 10 weeks until 8 September when Italy signed a peace. On the 9th a German patrol took over our camp. We moved to Mantua on a football ground. Each day the Jerries were bringing in our lads who were working on farms. When the place was full, 1,300, we were put in trucks en route for Germany.

On the day after the Germans struck PG 49 and PG 55, it was the turn of PG 29, to the west, in the province of Piacenza. On the eve of the Armistice it held 206 officers and 62 orderlies.

The camp at Veano in the hills between the Trebbia and Nure valleys was housed in the Villa Alberoni, a summer home for seminary students. It opened on 1 May 1942 for officers of field rank, majors and colonels, but more junior officers also had to be accommodated following Axis successes in North Africa.

Conditions were similar to those at Fontanellato, though relations were less harmonious owing to repeated escape attempts. However, when 'on 10 September information was received the Germans were approaching the camp,' the Italian commandant, Colonel Cornaggia Medici Castiglioni, cooperated with the British SBO, Colonel George Younghusband. Captors and captives scattered into the countryside. The Germans fired random shots into the surrounding woods, looted the stores and failed to capture a single prisoner.

Finally, the troops targeted a camp for Yugoslav officers, PG 26 at Cortemaggiore along the Via Emilia. The Germans succeeded in capturing some of the prisoners, but there were many escapes and several of the men became noted partisans.

Other prisons where Italians aided the POWs escape included PG 54 Fara-in-Sabina, PG 102 Aquila and PG 145

Campotosto. The guards also disappeared in several main camps and at most work camps. Some 50,000 Allied prisoners of war were able to flee into the countryside.

*

On 12 September 1943 the Germans rescued the deposed dictator Benito Mussolini from what he described as 'the highest prison in the world,' a ski lodge in the Gran Sasso mountain range. He was installed at Salò on Lake Garda and proclaimed the *Repubblica Sociale Italiana (RSI)*. It controlled the greater part of Italy, the German-occupied area north of the Gustav Line.

A week after the Armistice, the Germans issued a decree: 'Anyone who gives food and shelter or provides civilian clothes to British or American prisoners will face the severest penalties before the Tribunal of War.' In practice the sanctions included the burning of helpers' houses, deportation and execution by firing squad.

On 23 September a German proclamation offered a reward of twenty pounds sterling or 1,800 lire to anyone who recaptured a British or American escaped prisoner of war and handed them over to a troop detachment or headquarters.

The first military decree of the new Fascist republic on 10 October also made aiding and abetting the enemy a capital offence.

The response of most Italians to threats and bribes from Germans and Fascists was to redouble their efforts to help the escaped prisoners of war in every way possible, as we shall see in the next chapter.

6

THE HUSSARS

A quartet of Hussars from Fontanellato found shelter on a little farm on the Stirone torrent, only a day's march from the camp. One of them wrote about their experiences and was kind and helpful to me when starting my research.

Twenty-eight-year-old Lieutenant John (Jack) Andrew Comyn had been commissioned into the 8th King's Royal Irish Hussars in 1935 after Wellington College and Sandhurst. His family were Anglo-Irish and lived at Deans Grove, Wimborne, Dorset. The lieutenant was captured by the Italians on Sofafi Ridge, near Sidi Barrani, Egypt, on 10 December 1940. It was his first day as troop commander and his tank took a direct hit.

The officer was to spend the next four years and two months in six prisoner of war camps, three in Italy, three in Germany, but it was PG 49 that he described as 'undoubtedly the most pleasant POW camp I ever encountered.' It was the only one that he ever revisited.

Jack Comyn was in a group of 16 cavalry and rifle men who left the Rovacchia at dusk on 10 September. They thought that if they avoided towns and German lines of communication they would be certain to link up with the Allies. Landings were said to be imminent 60 miles away at La Spezia. Comyn related: 'Many months later we learned that these reports, emanating from the BBC, were put out to deceive the Germans. They certainly deceived us.'

'The first problem was to get over the railway line and the Via Emilia,' Jack Comyn told me. 'There was quite a lot of German military traffic on the road and we had to wait for intervals to scramble across. I remember some nasty wire fences. After that we just headed west into the hills in darkness and covered about 16 miles that night.'

Towards noon next day, the escapers were introduced to a local landowner called Signor Palumbo by some disbanded Italian soldiers. He had spent over 20 years running a restaurant in Soho and greeted them in faultless Cockney.

The Italian offered to arrange shelter for the escapers on local farms. Along with three other 8th Hussars, Jack Comyn was allocated to that of Ernesto Regalli (whom he called Regalo). Aged about 30, he had a wife and young twin daughters. Comyn recalled: 'Above his little holding was woodland and below the farmhouse the land dropped gently towards the Stirone, beside which ran a country road down the valley.'

The 8th Hussars party consisted, in order of seniority, of Captain Patrick (Pat) Howard Voltelin de Cleremont, Captain Comyn (newly promoted on 29 August), Lieutenant Charles Hedley, the eldest, and Second Lieutenant Donald Lewis Astley-Cooper, the youngest. Rank still mattered because they had been trained to follow the decisions of the senior officer, even in these unusual circumstances.

Patrick de Cleremont, aged 33, was the future commander of the regiment and recipient of the DSO in Korea for 'valiant and distinguished service.' Educated at Harrow and Sandhurst, he was recalled from the Reserve List in 1939 and served in the Western Desert. After acting as adjutant and twice being Mentioned in

Despatches, the captain was captured during the Battle of Sidi Rezegh in November 1941, together with many other Hussars. Jack Comyn had known Patrick de Cleremont before the war and described him as a kind and generous character, renowned in the regiment for his sardonic wit and as a bon viveur.

Charles Hedley had already been a soldier for 25 years. He was commissioned Quartermaster in the Field in 1940. The lieutenant had been captured near Bir Hacheim in May 1942. Patrick de Cleremont recalled: 'His stories of his experiences of echelon running in the Western Desert, of his many narrow escapes from delivering rations to the wrong side and his own capture with the Regimental Rum were famous in the Officers' Mess after the port had circulated.' Jack Comyn wrote that Hedley was 'a little Lancashire man, extremely able, of great but modest charm and possessing a wonderful sense of humour.'

Donald Astley-Cooper, aged 22 in September 1943, came from a titled service family. The second lieutenant had only joined the regiment in May 1940, but Jack Comyn had got to know him well at Fontanellato, where he played the clarinet in his band. Comyn remembered him as a shy but charming young man and a great athlete.

In 1994 Major Comyn wrote and privately circulated a small book of his wartime experiences called *Episodes*. He sent me this fascinating account of the Hussars' stay on the Stirone:

> At La Trinità we slept in the barn, the sweet smelling hay pleasant to the senses in those warm September nights, and came into the farmhouse for meals and to spend the evening. The Regalo family could not have been kinder hosts. Each morning the *Signora* would make fresh pasta, ladling out the flour from a wooden chest onto the kitchen table, mixing and kneading it and then cutting it into strips, *tagliatelle*! The pasta

would be cooked in the huge cauldron which hung permanently above the wood fire in the large open hearth. At the side stood a small iron stand above a little fire of glowing charcoal. On this the sauce would be cooked, using tomatoes, onions and snippets of liver or bacon. Inset deep into the thick stone wall beside the hearth was a large oven, closed with an iron door. This would be filled with a mass of twigs, which would be lit, allowed to burn until the interior of the oven was hot and then raked out. Into the oven would go freshly kneaded loaves, or sometimes a rabbit or a chicken. In the evenings our pasta would be washed down with the Regalos' own red wine, only just made and tasting abominably of the sulphur with which the vines had been sprayed.

Like all the *contadini* [peasants] we met later, the Regalos were then far from well off for food, and four extra mouths would have severely strained their resources if it had not been for Signor Palumbo, our Lady Bountiful. Every now and then he would send up to the farm a horse and cart carrying flour, salami, ham, cheese and wine and sometimes a chicken. His generosity was amazing and I am glad that I was able to visit him after the war and repay a little of it. On that occasion he told me that during the war he had always anticipated catastrophe and had laid in stocks of food. He had even hidden quantities of grain in the walls of his house.

We seemed to be in no danger from the Germans. From the farm there was an excellent view of the little road down the valley and we could soon vanish into the woods above us when a car was seen, as occasionally happened, usually Germans looking for fresh fruit and vegetables or wine. But there was a risk, feared by

Ernesto, that our presence might be betrayed by a *spia*, a local with Fascist or German sympathies. By day we exposed ourselves as little possible. Such diversions as we could arrange occurred after dark. Hugh Hope, who had helped me with my escape attempt at Fontanellato, was at a farm only half a mile away, together with Derek Hornsby, another 60th Rifleman, and we frequently met. At Borla, a tiny village just up the valley, there was a widow with English connections who once or twice entertained us to an excellent evening meal in her cosy cottage.

Palumbo put us in touch with neighbours of his, Manlio Carloni and his wife, a charming young couple who lived in a modern flat just outside the little town of Fidenza. They would sometimes ask us to stay, two at a time. This was quite an adventure. Fidenza lay some six miles down the little Torrente Stirone. We would set off after dark, not using the road but walking down the dry riverbed. Nearing Fidenza there would be a whistle from bushes on the bank and Manlio would appear to lead us to his home. There we enjoyed the luxury of a hot bath, excellent food and comfortable beds. All next day we would remain indoors, keeping quiet in response to Manlio's warnings that the inhabitants of the flat below were *Fascisti*. After dark we would return by the same route to La Trinità. Some years later I visited Manlio and his wife and was amused to receive the same injunction not to speak too loud, this time because the people below were *Comunisti*. I suspect that both warnings derived from nothing more than Italian love of intrigue.

One evening we were summoned to a secret meeting in a stone hut high in the woods. There we found a small party of young men all dressed in what appeared to be cowboy kit. It transpired that they were members of the dance band of a smart hotel in the spa town of Salsomaggiore, not far away. The object of the meeting was to set up a partisan group. There was a lot of talk, wine and laughter, but little was achieved except agreement for a further meeting. We turned up on the appointed evening, but they did not appear and we never saw them again.

It was with the Regalos that I first realised how severely deficient was my Italian, obtained only from books, because I had had little opportunity of conversation. An added difficulty was that the peasants spoke only in dialect. I was later to find that the dialect varied considerably in every region, practically every valley, of Italy. Instead of *'andiamo a casa'* (let's go home), Ernesto would say *'andoom a ca.'* And for *'vino'* he would use the French word *'vin.'* In spite of this he and I got on well and I was impressed by how hard he worked. Everywhere in north and central Italy the *contadini* were up at 4am to start the day.

Ernesto had his little relaxations. One afternoon he beckoned me to follow him up into the woods. He was carrying a spade, nothing unusual because there were no privies on Italian farms, all had to be returned to the land. When we stopped he dug a hole and extracted a large flagon of genuine Chianti. We spent the whole afternoon there. As he explained to me, he had sometimes to get away from the family. Ernesto also possessed a ready wit. On one occasion he was requisitioned by the local mayor to accompany a group of German officers who wanted to shoot. A hare was wounded, and Ernesto sent to find it. He found it, but instead of delivering it to the Germans hid it in a ditch. That evening we ate delicious hare stew. It was only when we had finished that Ernesto told us how he obtained it. 'There you are,' he ended. 'That is typical of this war. The German shoots the hare, the Italian steals it and the English eat it.'

Weeks went by and it was now mid October. There had been no further talk of a landing in the north of Italy and clearly both the Allied armies were heavily involved with the Germans south of Rome. We talked of getting to Switzerland, but we knew that the Swiss were interning escapees. Wengen was not a bad place to be interned, on parole and free to ski (as many found) but internment meant taking no further part in the war. A journey through occupied France to neutral Spain might be feasible, alternatively a junction with Tito in Yugoslavia. But we now knew that we could get help from the Italians and my inclination was to move south in the hope of getting through to our own armies fighting there.

Pat de Cleremont did not share my view. He thought we were well off where we were and should wait further. This was awkward as he was the Senior Officer. I sounded out Donald Astley-Cooper. He was of my opinion. One evening there was a somewhat acrimonious meeting at which Pat eventually agreed to our departure. Charlie Hedley later took me aside. 'I think you are right, Jarck (as he always pronounced my name), and I would love to come with you. But I might slow you up and anyway someone must stay with Pat.' So he did. In fairness to Pat's judgement, he and Charlie stayed put all that winter and in the spring moved south. After the fall of Rome in June 1944 they were freed by the oncoming Allies and got home long before me.

Donald and I set off southward up through the woods

behind the farm. We had a map of Italy torn from a school atlas, somewhat lacking in detail. For the first mile Ernesto guided us. *'Pian, piano,'* [Easy does it] he kept saying. 'If you try to go at this pace you will never get over the mountains.' Then we parted.

After leaving the Stirone, Captain Comyn and Second Lieutenant Astley-Cooper travelled down a large part of the peninsula. Every evening they would approach a lonely farmhouse, say who they were and ask to be received. Only on two occasions was hospitality refused. Money was never offered and never requested. The officers would leave a note asking the Allies to recognise what their hosts had done for them.

By 28 November the pair had reached the battle zone on the River Sangro. They decided to push on through the snow until contact was made with British forces. After walking for 24 hours, the Hussars were forced by mist and low cloud to seek shelter in a shepherd's hut near Opi. There were three other fugitives inside. Suddenly, there was the rattle of automatic fire and a shout: 'Look out, the Jerries are coming!'

The servicemen were recaptured. Jack Comyn related: 'It was the most miserable point in my life … It was horrifying to find oneself a prisoner of war again after such an effort.' The duo were deported and spent the rest of the war in German camps. They were liberated on 12 April 1945 from *Oflag* 79 Brunswick by the Americans.

Like many of the ex-prisoners of war in Italy, Major Comyn revisited the people and places he had got to know so well when on the run. In his case this was in the early 1980s:

I saw Ernesto once again, ten years ago. La Trinità was by then an abandoned ruin, like so many hill farms in Italy. Ernesto and his wife, both much aged, had a small modern house, with a patch of vineyard, in Borla. He opened a bottle of wine and we talked. One of the twins was married, the other a nurse in Swansea. He told me that they had looked after many other escapers after my departure. I had an uncomfortable feeling that of me he had little recollection, although he clearly remembered Hugh Hope, who had been to see him soon after the war.

Major Hope, aged 29 in September 1943, was educated at Eton and Worcester College Oxford. His home was Pinkie House, Musselburgh, then in Midlothian. A regular soldier in the King's Royal Rifle Corps, the major was a holder of the Military Cross.

Jack Comyn told me: 'Hugh Hope set off south on his own, speaking no Italian, and got through the lines successfully.' The major had been given shelter, together with Lieutenant Hornsby, on a farm at Aione, a stockbreeding area higher up the valley.

The officers left on 18 October when the adjacent holding was raided and a Yugoslav captain recaptured. The major crossed the River Sangro near Castel di Sangro and reached the British lines on 21 November. He eventually rejoined his regiment in Italy. Lieutenant Hornsby went north and had already escaped to Switzerland.

*

Captain de Cleremont and Lieutenant Hedley, the two officers from the 8th Kings Royal Irish Hussars who decided to stay on the Parma-Piacenza border after the departure of their friends, remained in enemy territory for more than a year.

The pair became friendly with two Italians, Olimpio Dolci, aged 48, and his sister, Maria, the widow of Signor Lusignani.

They lived together on a farm on the western edge of the hamlet of La Trinità, which is situated on a hill overlooking the Stirone.

Maria had brought the officers meals of pasta, bread, cheese and wine when they first came to the valley. Captain de Cleremont sent letters of thanks in French, as Olimpio had worked in France before the war. In the messages, the captain referred to two other officer escapers who were being sheltered by the priest of Borla, Don Angelo Lambrini, saying that it was not possible for them to join the party at the Regallis. It would overburden the house and the locality.

In August and September 1944 Lieutenant Hedley wrote letters confirming the help given to them by Olimpio and Maria, which are typical of the many thousands of testimonials that were left with Italian helpers:

To whom it may concern: Olimpio Dolci

This is to certify that the above named has rendered valuable assistance to British Officers and other ranks for a long period.

He assisted me and seven other officers in September, October and November 1943 and since that time has had in his care five South African soldiers, finding them refuge during a most difficult period. He is the brother of Maria Lusignani, who is also in possession of proof of her valuable assistance to us. We hope that his work will be recognised and rewarded, as he has been a most valuable ally.

To British or Allied HQ in Italy: Maria Lusignani

This is to certify that the above named has rendered invaluable assistance to British ex-POWs ever since the Armistice. She has, to my knowledge, given food and shelter to a large number of officers and men who have passed through the area. The fact that she was constantly under Fascist supervision by reason of her known pro-British views has not deterred her in any way and she has run the gravest risks in continuing her help to all who were in need.

She assisted me and seven other officers for several weeks in September and October last year.

I hope and trust that her work on our behalf will receive the recognition it so richly deserves and that she and her property will receive due consideration when British or Allied troops occupy the area.

Her door is still open at this most difficult period when so many others, for fear of reprisals, have withdrawn their assistance. She is a widow, maiden name 'Zoli', Zelinda Maria, and one of the stoutest hearted women I have ever had the good fortune to meet.

The Stirone Valley had been swamped by a tide of escaped prisoners of war making for the mountains. Olimpio and Maria recalled that there were continuous arrivals and departures at their house. One night they gave food and shelter to 15 escapers on their small farm, one of the many sizeable parties at large immediately after the flight from PG 49.

Over a three-month period the Dolcis shared the task with three other farmers of providing food and lodging for eight British officers. In addition to the two Hussars, they included three more escapers from Fontanellato: lieutenants John Forrest Taylor and John William Burman of the Royal Tank Regiment and Kenneth Noel Sutcliffe from the Royal Artillery. Six South African soldiers were also given food and shelter for a week and food twice a week for a month. In addition,

Olimpio acted as a local guide, directing escapers across the mountains towards the Ceno Valley and Bardi.

Captain de Cleremont and Lieutenant Hedley moved between farms in the Vigoleno area within the commune of Vernasca. They usually travelled by night and slept in haylofts and outbuildings to make it appear less incriminating for their hosts.

My mother, Clara, brought the two Hussars supplies from Castell'Arquato. Captain de Cleremont sent her this letter by courier on Wednesday, 22 March 1944:

My dear Signorina,

So many thanks for the parcel of such useful things, they will be invaluable.

It would give me great pleasure to meet you here on Sunday, April 2nd. I shall come after dark about 7.30pm.

I hope this will suit you. I am on my way out on a *giro* [excursion] and shall be returning at the end of next week.

I look forward to seeing you then.

Sincerely yours,
Patrick de Cleremont

Other helpers included Antonio Lusci, Giuseppe Illica, Signor Ruggi and Miss Tina Valenta. The officers stayed at her farmstead for odd days over the months and on 9 June made it their permanent base. The officers remained there until 25 October, when they began the journey south.

After three days march, the pair linked up with a party hoping to cross enemy lines. It was led by 57-year-old

Lieutenant Colonel Henry Lowry-Corry, MC, from the Royal Artillery, commander of the 67th Regiment at Tobruk and escaper from PG 29 Veano. His group included Major JE Fairleigh of the Indian Army and another officer from PG 49, Lieutenant Edward Raeburn, also from the Royal Artillery.

The escapers left the Rossano Valley on 28 October 1944 and spent a week covering a distance as the crow flies of 51 miles. It involved over 39 hours of marching, climbing and clambering. On 3 November the party neared Ruosina, seven miles south east of Massa, and made contact with a black soldier of the United States 92nd Infantry Division.

The two Hussars returned to England in December. The following spring, they rejoined the regiment in time to take part in the Rhine Crossing and the Victory Parade in Berlin.

*

After the war, Jack Comyn was posted to the Vienna Headquarters of British-Troops-in-Austria (BTA). For his private transport he purchased a famous Rolls Royce from a Church of Scotland minister, GRW 59, a 20/25 drop-head coupe.

Jack Comyn left the army in 1950 with the rank of major. He retired three decades later after farming in Ireland and Essex. In 1968 the major was appointed MBE. In the early 1980s he revisited the former camp at Fontanellato, as he recalled: 'My wife Elizabeth and I went there some years ago and were courteously shown around by the nuns, now firmly re-established in their rightful domain. We trod the marble stairs that I remembered, and agreed that it had been quite a palatial residence for prisoners of war.'

The remaining three Hussars served in the Korean War (1950-1953). Donald Astley-Cooper was promoted to captain and commanded an armoured group of Cromwell tanks known as Cooper Force. He was killed on 3 January 1951 in the Battle of Koyang. His last radio message was: 'It's bloody rough!' He was never heard from again.

After leading 'A' Squadron in Korea and receiving the DSO, Patrick de Cleremont took over command of the 8th Hussars at the barracks in Lüneburg, Germany. He retired three years later with the rank of lieutenant colonel and enjoyed country pursuits from a large house on the River Tweed.

Following his service in Germany, Charles Hedley left the army with the rank of Major (QM), after 35 years service. He was appointed Member of the British Empire (MBE) and retired to Southern Australia.

*

Major Jack Comyn wrote to me in January 2000: 'I can never forget or repay the outstanding help and support we all received from the Italian people ... I do not think that these ever received the thanks and recognition they deserved. I am most interested to learn that your family was among them.'

When we were discussing the little house on the Stirone where he and his three friends had been sheltered after they left the camp, I always had the feeling that it might have been one of those my mother visited to help escapers.

At Easter-time in 2009 I set out with two of my ex-partisan friends, Luigi Sesenna and Gaetano (Mino) Avogadri, to follow this lost trail. The farm was south of the river and said to be abandoned. Could we locate it and find out more? We travelled by car up the Stirone Valley, along the main road from the plain. The escapers had followed the same route on foot.

The innkeeper in the village of Borla told us that Ernesto Regalli's son Claudio had been in that very morning and that we might be able to find him on his land across the valley. We went down to the river and across the bridge to the commune of Pellegrino and the province of Parma. We drove 600 metres upstream to a point where the Stirone enters a small gorge at the foot of a thickly wooded slope.

We were delighted to see a figure wearing an anorak and baseball cap in the fields. He was tilling the soil in the pouring rain. We introduced ourselves and told Claudio of our quest. He climbed into Mino's Volkswagen to talk in the dry.

Claudio, in his early sixties, had the weathered complexion and firm handshake of a countryman. He told us that the family farmstead was sold years ago. It has been replaced by the impressive villa a hundred metres above us on the hillside, which was built for people from Milan. He has retained the land between the road and the stream, where he cultivates an orchard and grows vegetables.

Claudio added that as well as his father and mother and four children, the farm had been home to his mother's parents and her younger sister. His grandfather, Partemio Solari, had been a restaurateur in London before the war, like my grandfather, and so was able to talk to the escapers in English.

I had been trying to discover the identity of a farmer with this Christian name for over a year. Family friends Giulia and Emma Guarnieri told me how they accompanied my mother through La Trinità and down across the Stirone to take supplies to a farm where two escapers were sheltering. The route was via Monte La Ciocca in Vernasca, except once when there were Germans there. The girls had looked for the men after an enemy roundup, but they had disappeared. The farmer's name had been Partemio.

Claudio also revealed that his aunt, who is called Eva and now lives in Germany, had married one of the escapers whom his family had sheltered on the farm. He was Sub-Conductor Victor Rolland, a warrant officer in the Indian Army who was of French origin. Like most of the escapers in the area, he too had come from the camp at Fontanellato.

I knew the name well. Victor was one of the prisoners with whom my mother was in regular contact and my grandfather had provided him with a suit and other items. This is an early letter the soldier sent to my mother from the farm:

Dear Miss C.,

I thank you very much indeed for the so useful articles which I have received from you: handkerchiefs, smoker's outfit, combs and the bottle of *vino*, etc. All at a time when I did happen to be in need of those very things. They have been very much appreciated I assure you.

Yours gratefully,
Vittorio.

Claudio told us that Victor had managed to avoid recapture and that he had remained in the area until the liberation. The happy couple went to live in Wales, moving to Holland some years later.

With our thanks ringing in his ears, Claudio got out of the car and returned to his land and the rain. As we drove back towards the main road, I conjured up an image of the escapers, my mother as a student and the other helpers in this quiet, little valley.

The spell was broken by Mino asking: 'Would you like to go back to Castell'Arquato or directly to Fiorenzuola station?' I was returning by train to Milan that night. If only things had been so simple all those years ago.

7

SANCTUARY

The hamlet of La Trinità, overlooking the Stirone, provided sanctuary to many escapers. Amongst the helpers was Olimpio Dolci's foster brother, Pietro Guarnieri. He shared the passion for aiding escaped prisoners of war with my grandfather, Alfredo Dall'Arda, a close friend. They had grown up together in the little village of Chiavenna Rocchetta and afterwards lived on the same road in Castell'Arquato. My family was at number 8 and the Guarnieris at 16 on Via Guglielmo Marconi, a level country road running from the river bridge at the bottom of the village towards the sleepy hamlet of Vigolo Marchese.

Pietro was a *mediatore*, a country go-between who would organise the sale of anything from a patch of land to a herd of cattle. Together with a Signor Rossetti, he also rented a creamery from Olimpio at La Trinità for the production of butter and provolone cheese. It was located alongside the local mill (now replaced by a villa) on the gentle slopes between the Dolci farm and the Stirone. When the German troops came they stole everything.

Between September 1943 and May 1944 Pietro gave

meals to those he described as 'British prisoners in transit.' He also provided money to another officer from Fontanellato, Lieutenant Costas Jacovides of the Cyprus Regiment.

At the end of the war Pietro recalled:

> I live in Castell'Arquato but rent a small creamery at Trinità di Borla. In the very many journeys I made, I carried money, clothing and cigarettes to the prisoners. All these items were provided by friends of mine from Castell'Arquato. As a result, I also came under suspicion from the Fascist Police, but was warned in time and was able to hide.
>
> I gave money, bread and wine and carried all the material given by Mrs Filomena Scaglioni and Mr Dall'Arda. For all these reasons, I had to stay in the mountains for more than a year, because the Republicans had decided to shoot me.

The escapers in the area included several men from prison camps other than Fontanellato. Three soldiers received help from five different farmers over a three-month period. The fugitives were: Driver Wallace H Harris, Royal Army Service Corps, from West Hallam, near Ilkeston, Derbyshire, Gunner SB Baines, Royal Artillery, and Lance Corporal R Shand, Royal Engineers, from Aberdeen.

After providing hospitality to Lieutenant Langrishe's group shortly after the Armistice, Alberto Sanini gave food to the three soldiers in October 1943 on his farm at Vigoleno.

Farmer Stefano Granelli, just downstream from La Trinità at La Villa, recalled that in November and December he provided chickens, bread and milk to the three men every other day and that they lived in the woods.

His neighbour, Ernesto Varani, said that he gave Corporal Shand and Driver Harris soup most evenings and milk in the morning. They were suffering from malarial fever and he obtained medicine to treat them, mended their shoes and had their laundry done. The soldiers' hideout was on the same side of the stream as the Regalli farm, and so in the commune of Pellegrino Parmense.

Gunner Baines spent three days with Olimpio and Maria Dolci. Driver Harris and Lance Corporal Shand were sheltered for three weeks in October in the hayloft of farmers Antonio Solari and his wife Dina. Antonio spoke English, having worked in London before the war.

It would be nice for the story of the three soldiers to have a happy ending. However, they were eventually recaptured and sent to camps in Greater Germany: Driver Harris was at *Stalag* 4C Wistritz bei Teplitz, and Lance Corporal Shand and Gunner Baines at *Stalag* 4D Torgau (Elbe).

The Solaris also fed and sheltered two officers from Fontanellato in their house for a total of 30 days over the period December 1943 to the end of March 1944. They were lieutenants William Benzie and John William Burman from the Royal Tank Regiment. Four other homesteads also looked after these officers in turn.

Hussar captain Patrick de Cleremont wrote a letter confirming that Signor Solari had been of great help to Driver Harris and Lance Corporal Shand when they first came to the area. They had spent a week's shelter on the farm and received food and wine.

In another testimonial, lieutenants Benzie and Burman wrote: 'Antonio Solari and his wife have fed, housed and given a bed to the two undersigned POWs from *Campo* PG No. 49 Fontanellato. They cannot be too highly praised for their kindness and the warmth of their welcome.'

At the end of the war, the priest at Borla, Don Angelo Lambrini, who had also sheltered escaped prisoners, completed and witnessed many of the forms sent by his parishioners to the Allied Screening Commission.

★

In 2008 I revisited La Trinità, the first port of call for many of the prisoners of war from PG 49, together with my two ex-partisan friends, Luigi and Mino.

The village is on a hillside overlooking the left bank of the Stirone. Houses and barns, a small church and an inn, hug the contours of the winding country road. The turrets of Vigoleno castle peep between hills further down the valley. It is a peaceful place.

On the slopes just below the village, the mill and the creamery, which was run by Pietro Guarnieri and his partner Rossetti, have long since gone, replaced by a large modern villa and outbuildings. The old mule track to Borla, along which the servicemen trudged towards the mountains, has been widened and asphalted.

In wartime there were only a few houses. Many new ones have been built and older ones restored, frequently by returned emigrants. But there are fewer people, owing to the drift to the cities. Dwellings are often second homes, even if the owners frequently have local connections.

This is a hunting area and the escapers always commented on the barking of dogs that followed them from farm to farm. We attracted the attention of their noisy descendants, who were tethered on long chains.

We called in at the inn, which is well known in the area for its good food. When I told our story and mentioned the names of the helpers, the lady proprietor said that Antonio

Solari was her uncle and that she lives in Olimpio and Maria Dolci's old house.

The dwelling, which my mother visited regularly with money and supplies for escapers, stands on the last curve of the road through the village before it meanders into the mountains. The house was damaged at the end of the war and had to be substantially rebuilt.

The restaurateur recommended that we meet her father, Gino Rizzi, still a cattle dealer at 87, who is Dina Solari's brother. After a good meal, we found him in his house nearby. Gino told us that he served in the *Alpini* (mountain troops) during the war, but as he was the only son was stationed at Piacenza instead of on the border at Bardonecchia, and so saw what was going on at home.

He told us stories of the wartime escapers and we walked together to the small abandoned house at the top of his field where the Solaris hid some of the men. It is said to be the oldest dwelling in La Trinità.

As in wartime, the stone building is still divided vertically into two unequal sections. One part is owned by Gino and the other by his neighbours on Antonio and Dina Solari's old farm. The couple's farmhouse has been replaced by a large new one with spacious outbuildings.

The families from the farm and the surrounding houses came out to talk to us. They offered us something to drink. 'You see what good people they are,' said Luigi. 'Without their help during the war, our cause would have been lost.'

The farmers readily agreed to show us the escapers' hiding place. We plodded past ancient apple trees in blossom, the heavy, dark earth sodden underfoot after rain.

In wartime the upstairs of the abandoned house was a hayloft. A wooden ladder was used by the escapers to gain access to the top floor, which they would pull up after them.

Wine was stored in the cool of the basement.

The soldiers would join the Solaris for meals in the evening and many a boisterous hour was spent in talking about the war and happy times to come.

8

SECRET JOURNEY

The solidarity between many Italians and the Allied servicemen was part of a humanitarian impulse that swept the nation after the Armistice. South of the Stirone torrent in the province of Parma most of the escaped prisoners of war were sheltered in the Fidenza–Salsomaggiore–Pellegrino area, which was also the focus of early partisan activity and support for disbanded Italian troops.

Following the fighting between the former Axis partners, the Germans ordered all Italian soldiers to report to their barracks or be treated as deserters. At Fidenza, the nearest large town to Fontanellato, soldiers of the 33rd Tank Regiment were rounded up and taken to the railway station for deportation to Germany. Railway workers and townspeople quickly found everyday clothes for the captives and helped many of them to escape. Meanwhile, the castle garrison was looted by young men looking for weapons and by women and children seeking more everyday pickings. The angry Germans fired on onlookers in the square. A woman died next day from her injuries.

Soon after the escape from Fontanellato on 9 September, about 150 escaped prisoners of war flooded into towns and villages on the plain. They were given civilian clothing, money and supplies by the anti-Fascists. Gino Fantoni of Parola paid for many of the men to be taken to the Salsomaggiore hills in the taxi of Gino Albignani (Canali). He had been evacuated with his family to Paroletta and became the driver of the Resistance, carrying partisans to battles and leaders to meetings.

A discussion between Allied officers and representatives of the anti-Fascist Committee of Parma was held at Chiesa Bianca on 23 September with the aim of forming joint partisan units, but no agreement was reached. However, in a few cases Allied servicemen did join the rebels. British and American personnel also acted as intermediaries in arranging airdrops of weapons and supplies.

The local Resistance was mobilised by the Italian Communist Party, the PCI. Leaders such as Emilio Robuschi and Remo Polizzi worked tirelessly to create a network of dissidents in town and country. By 15 October the opposition was sufficiently well organised to create a provincial liberation committee, the CLN, in Parma. The Communists were joined by representatives of the Christian Democrat, Liberal, Republican, and Action parties.

At the end of September, the Communist party had issued a blueprint for the partisan struggle. The Parma Valley was chosen as an area in which to recruit and train detachments. Attacks were to be concentrated in the Taro Valley, along the state highway of the Cisa and against the railway between Fornovo and Pontremoli (about 56 kilometres) on the Parma to La Spezia line.

The Ceno Valley was selected as an area where escapers would be sheltered and given assistance to rejoin friendly forces. Guides were provided to take the fugitives to Bardi, the old town on a rocky outcrop at the head of the valley.

It is an area with many links to South Wales through emigration. First to welcome the servicemen was the prefect Francesco Berni.

The liberation committee of the town of Fornovo in the Taro Valley, to the east, also played an important role in helping the Allied escapers. On 20 September the committee was contacted by Lazzaro Bazzoni from Mariano in the commune of Pellegrino. Several fugitives from Fontanellato had arrived and were in urgent need of food and clothing. Despite shortages and the threats by the Germans against anyone helping escapers, the committee had obtained enough items for Bazzoni to make the first distribution within five days. The Resistance even arranged with butcher Dallatomasina for the fugitives to be fed on meat taken from the daily ration assigned to the German soldiers stationed in Fornovo. The assistance continued over the winter.

On 8 March 1944 the first successful partisan group was created at Ceriato in the Iggio Valley, named Copelli after a fallen comrade. They ambushed a *Carabiniere* car and released a prisoner at Scipione on the way to La Trinità. On 18 March, in their 'baptism of fire,' the partisans attacked the garrison at Pellegrino, made up of *Carabinieri* and forest guards. Rebels also halted the Lugagnano-Bardi bus.

The Germans issued a proclamation to the people of Fidenza on 18 April warning of the severest consequences for engaging in rebellion or spreading false rumours. Spies were also active in the commune. A local priest, Don Lorenzo Guareschi, was denounced and imprisoned. Lawyer and CLN member Manlio Bonatti was deported to Germany.

This spiral of partisan activity and swift reaction by the authorities made the Fidenza-Salsomaggiore-Pellegrino area too dangerous for the escaped prisoners of war. On 10 April one of the orderlies from Fontanellato lost his life.

Trooper John Harrison, aged 27, of the 7th Queen's Own Hussars, Royal Armoured Corps, from Belfast in Northern Ireland, had been sheltered at Mariano for four months. Two days later, an unknown Allied soldier, believed to have been a Scot, fell in battle at Pontenceno.

Other escapers from PG 49 in the area included captains John Baddeley, John Fairbrass and John Moore, and lieutenants John Ballantyne, William Benzie, Richard Brooke, EJD Bruen, John Burman, FG Cook, Peter Holworthy, Kenneth Sutcliffe, John Taylor and Jack Younger. Twelve different helpers sheltered Lieutenant Taylor in turn, including Giacomo Ziveri at Bardi, whose house was burnt down by the Germans as a reprisal.

The Fornovo CLN received a warning note from Signor Bazzoni. It read: 'A reliable informant has told me that the Republican police are aware that Britons are being sheltered in the Mariano area. They must leave immediately.' Some of the soldiers wanted to go to the Bardi or Bedonia areas in the mountains to the south west, while the remainder had chosen a journey north to Milan and the crossing to Switzerland. This group would be looked after by the comrades in Fidenza with whom Bazzoni was in contact.

Lieutenant John Taylor of the Royal Tank Regiment, known to everyone as 'Big John' as he was well over six feet tall, had to remain at Mariano through illness. He eventually escaped.

The following evening, the CLN sent a car belonging to the Lombatti Company to meet Signor Bazzoni and two escapers at Viazzano. They were taken on board a train under the noses of Germans and Fascist militia by hiding them amongst a crowd of partisans. Signor Bazzoni accompanied the escapers as far as the Bedonia area.

The ultimate decision to repatriate the prisoners in the mountains was taken by the liberation committee in Parma.

Emilio Robuschi found safe houses for several of the fugitives in Fidenza while arrangements were made to obtain railway tickets and false documents. A key helper was Guido Camorali, whose home was near the railway station. He was one of 72 partisans who lost their lives in the commune during the liberation struggle.

Two of the escapers were lieutenants William Benzie and John Burman from the 42nd Battalion, Royal Tank Regiment. They had been captured on 5 June 1942 during an unsuccessful counter-offensive south of Gazala in north eastern Libya. It was the turning point of the battle. After transfer to Italy, the pair spent six months at transit camp PG 66 Capua, before moving to PG 17 Rezzanello and finally PG 49.

William Benzie, aged 33 in September 1943, was an energetic man with a great sense of humour. He was the eldest of five children of a City of Glasgow policeman and his wife. The young man found employment in the drapery trade and then became a professional footballer, until being called up when war was declared. After initial training, he went to Sandhurst and was commissioned in October 1940. The regiment would soon be sent to North Africa.

On 5 June 1942, William Benzie related, 'We attacked German positions about 06.00 hours. We met strong opposition and my tank was knocked out. The German tanks went through us and I was captured by their support infantry.'

The officers regularly crossed into the province of Piacenza, using the safe houses along the Stirone on the way. Several letters sent by John Burman to my relatives survive. He came from Manchester and was the officer in charge of the boot repair shop at PG 49. The lieutenant was charismatic and learned to speak Italian well.

The earliest letter reads:

My Dear Miss Dall'Arda,

My friends and I cannot thank you sufficiently for the soap and cigarettes, which you have so kindly sent us. We can only say that when we return again we would be delighted to see and talk to you.

Thank you once again.

Yours very sincerely, for myself and friends,
John W Burman
Lt., RTR.

On the weekend of 8-9 April 1944 Lieutenant Burman stayed at my grandparents' house at 8, Via Guglielmo Marconi in Castell'Arquato. Next day he sent a message:

My very dear Mr and Mrs and Miss Dall'Arda,

May I place on record my sincerest thanks for the nicest and happiest weekend I have yet passed in Italy.

You cannot imagine just how marvellous it is to find oneself in pleasant and civilised surroundings after having spent nearly three years *in giro* [on the go].

I sincerely hope that I may repay your kind hospitality one day very soon, if not here, then at home.

Yours very sincerely,
John W Burman
Lieut. RTR

The officer also wrote to my mother on Sunday, 23 April:

Dear Miss -------,

I was sorry not to see you today, but I expect that you were unable to come because of all the trouble which took place yesterday.

However, I shall keep trying and will be at the big white stone on Sunday, May 7th at three o'clock old time.

Will you please bring with you the receipts which you wish to change and I will bring fresh ones with me, for all those which were altered or mutilated.

Also if you are able, please bring the rest of the money which you thought would be available.

Whatever happens I shall be there and I do hope that nothing occurs to stop us this time.

Please convey my kindest thoughts to your father and mother.

Yours very sincerely,
John Burman
Lt., RTR.

The money was to finance the prisoners' escape attempts. Eight received funds in March and April. Three of the men made successful escapes and the other five were ultimately recaptured.

John Burman never did keep his appointment with my mother. Four days after writing the letter, he had to take swift action to avoid recapture.

The officer's Escape Report reads:

We left camp 49 under the orders of Lieutenant Colonel de Burgh and then broke up into small parties. I left the area with Lieutenant William Benzie, 42nd Battalion Royal Tank Regiment, and remained with him for the rest of the period in Italy. We lived generally in the area of Mariano di Pellegrino, Parma, for this time. We contacted the 'partisans,' whom we discovered to be mostly of the 'bandit' type. We had nothing further to do with these people.

We were eventually put in touch with an organisation, which after many false alarms, managed to have us sent over the border via Fidenza, Milan and Lago Maggiore.

A guide arrived at the house of Lazzaro Bazzoni to take Captain J Moore, Lieutenant P Bruen and two other officers to Switzerland. As these four had gone back to the mountains for a short period, and were therefore unavailable, Lieutenant Benzie and I asked to go in their place.

We were taken by car to Fidenza, by rail to Milan, and from Milan to Laveno on Lago Maggiore. We crossed to Intra and walked to Brissago with guides. Their names were not given, nor those of the people in whose house we passed the afternoon in Milan whilst waiting for the train. There were two male and one female guides.

The length of the train journey from Fidenza to Milan is 107 kilometres, and Milan to Laveno, on the eastern shore of Lake Maggiore, another 72 kilometres. The men arrived in Switzerland on 29 April 1944.

Lieutenant William Benzie wrote in his Escape Report:

I was allowed to go free by the Italian Commandant. I lived for about eight months in the district of

Mariano, Pellegrino, Province of Parma, and was given food, shelter and clothing by the people of that area.

I travelled by train from Fidenza on 27.4.44 to Milan, from Milan to Laveno, crossed Lake Maggiore to Intra. On both parts of the journey I was escorted by a guide. At Intra I was handed over to the partisans and one of them acted as guide until I crossed the Swiss border at Brissago on 29.4.44.

I know very little of the organisation except that their work was handled by a man named Lazzaro Bazzoni, Casa Masaschi, Mariano, Pellegrino, Parma. This man did excellent work and was a tireless worker on behalf of British escaped POWs.

Another officer on the journey was Lieutenant Kenneth Noel Sutcliffe from the Royal Artillery. He had been captured on 29 June 1942. The regiment was attached to the 10th Indian Division, the main force in the Mersa Matruh fortress on the coast in north western Egypt, which was taken by Axis forces over three days. The lieutenant was captured at El-Daba on the road to El Alamein on the last day. It was the limit of the enemy advance.

In his Escape Report he recalled:

Having received little accurate information with reference to the embarkation of our own troops I moved west into the mountainous area between Parma and Genova, until November, attempted twice to move south by secure routes but I failed to contact a reliable guide.

In January I decided to wait for an offensive to open and then to move south. On 27.4.44 an organisation with which I had been in contact since December 1943 offered a guide to cross into Switzerland. This offer I accepted due to the reluctance of the local populace to shelter me for any further length of time.

From December 1943 until April 1944 I was in contact with British lieutenants: J Younger, Coldstream Guards; J Taylor, 7th Battalion, RTR; J Burman, RTR; and W Benzie, RTR.

On 28 April, accompanied by Lieutenant J Burman, RTR, and Lieutenant William Benzie, RTR, I left Fidenza (Parma) station for Milan under the guidance of Luigi Turconi who conducted us to a private house in Milan. The same evening, we left Milan by train for Laveno on Lake Maggiore, then by ferry across the lake to Intra-Verbania. From Intra we were guided by Sergio Catallape on foot over the mountains, crossing the frontier at 17.30 hours on 29 April 1944 at Brissago.

The guide on the train from Fidenza, Luigi Turconi, was a student activist. Lazzaro Bazzoni and his wife were shot in Milan in mysterious circumstances in March 1945.

Another of the Mariano group of escapers had succeeded in reaching Switzerland on 24 April, five days before his friends, following a short land route. Lieutenant Richard Neville Brooke from the 2nd Scots Guards was aged 28. The son of a baronet, he was captured at Rigel Ridge near 'Knightsbridge' in Libya on 13 June 1942. The lieutnant lived at Mariano with Lazzaro Bazzoni and Ida Papisca for seven months, together with Lieutenant Jack Younger. His Escape Report, unusually written in the third person, reads:

Camp 49 moved out in companies on 9.9.43 and the following night split up. Lieutenant Brooke, in company with Lieutenant JW Younger, moved to the vicinity of Pellegrino and lived in that locality till mid January, trying to get in touch with Italian partisans near Bedonia and living with them for about a fortnight and taking part in one operation which was a complete fiasco. Finding that the partisans were ineffective and unreliable, Lieutenant Brooke returned to Pellegrino and then contacted guides who took him to Switzerland by the following route: By train Fidenza to Luino, thence on foot to Ponte Tresa.

Guides from the Action Party took him by train from Fidenza to Milan and Varese and thence in a train to a small village only a mile from the frontier. Then by foot to the wire, under the wire where a small stream ran underneath it, across a river and thence to Ponte Tresa. A very easy, practical route.

Various private organisations were heard of which appeared to operate with varying success and most of which charged large sums for taking prisoners of war to Switzerland. The best appeared to be the Action Party, which was thoroughly well organised and cost nothing.

After the war, Richard Brooke became a prominent chartered accountant and in 1981 succeeded his father as the tenth Baronet Brooke of Norton Priory in the County of Chester.

The Milan section of the *Comitato di Liberazione Nazionale* (CLN), the new national Resistance movement, created the escape organisation in September 1943 on the orders of Ferruccio Parri of the Action Party. *The Ufficio Assistenza*

Prigionieri di Guerra Alleati (The Service for Assisting Allied Prisoners of War), commonly known as the Milan Network, sought to evacuate ex-prisoners of war, to sustain those unable to leave their hiding places and to contact individuals and groups able to give donations or assistance. Under the energetic direction of engineer Giuseppe Bacciagaluppi, the organisation helped 1,865 ex-prisoners to cross the 463-mile border with neutral Switzerland between September 1943 and March 1945: 1,297 from the Commonwealth, 313 Yugoslavs and 255 other allies.

When the undertaking went smoothly, it only took a day or two to transport the servicemen to the sanctuary of Switzerland. Vast sums were spent on rail travel, the purchase of cycles and boats and the services of professional guides, who were essential for the last leg of the journey. They were usually smugglers.

Allied prisoners of war escaping into neutral territory were technically free men under International Law, but following a gentleman's agreement between governments, the Allies agreed to the Swiss exercising a measure of military control over them.

The liberation of south eastern France by the Allied 7th Army in August 1944 opened up a land corridor. It would allow the repatriation of all the Allied servicemen by the end of the year.

Meanwhile, several thousand of their comrades were still marooned in Fascist Italy.

9

THE LIBERATED ZONES

High in the mountains of Parma province, the partisans were provided with weapons and supplies by Allied airdrops, which began in March 1944. On 10 June rebels of the 12th Garibaldi Brigade were able to occupy Bardi.

Six days earlier, three captured partisans had been executed by the Germans on the road to Varsi. The victims included an Australian escaped POW known to his comrades as 'Jak.' He was infantryman Jack Wilson, aged 34, from North Melbourne, Victoria. His companions were Aldo Fornasari and Luigi Evangelista, the 17-year-old son of the fruiterer in Castell'Arquato.

A public meeting was held in the square of the newly-liberated Bardi and lawyer Giuseppe Lumia was acclaimed as mayor. An organisation was formed to help Allied prisoners of war, the *Comitato Assistenziale fra gli ex prigionieri Britannici*. In his 1945 book, *Bardi Centrale di Patriotteria*, Lumia related that 40 escapers had been sheltered in the locality.

The partisans moved down the valley and the Free Zone of the Val Ceno was inaugurated. It covered 10 communes with a total population of about 40,000. On 26 June the Free

Territory of Taro was also created to the south, based around Borgotaro, Bedonia, Albareto, Compiano and Tornolo. The area covered 240 square kilometres and included important road and rail links with Liguria. Achille Pellizzari was chosen as prefect and he founded a partisan newspaper, *La Nuova Italia*.

The rebel forces united in a new division for the Ceno Valley and defeated two German attempts to reopen access to the coast at the end of June. However, on 8 July the Germans and the Fascist *Decima Mas* launched a large-scale offensive against the liberated zones. Savage reprisals were taken against the local population: 40 civilians were executed, including three priests, and the villages of Pessola and Strela were put to the torch. Bardi was taken on 17 July.

Over the summer, as the Germans lost ground in the centre of Italy and began to retreat north, Allied special missions and parachute drops to the partisans became more common. To the south east of Bardi a permanent mission of MI 9 was in operation in the second half of 1944 on Monte Barigazzo. Over the Cisa Pass in the Rossano Valley, Major Gordon Lett, one of the ex-prisoners of war from PG 29 Veano, led the International Battalion of partisans. On 27 July he was promoted to British Liaison Officer as head of Special Force Blundell Mission. A very successful escape line was created over the mountains. It ran through German 14th Army positions along the Gothic Line to United States 5th Army forces in the province of Lucca.

Meanwhile, several officers from Fontanellato had joined partisans in Parma Province. Captain Jack Baddeley of the Hampshire Regiment served with a detachment on Monte Barigazzo for two months and took part in the liberation of Bardi. When the Germans retook the free zone, he moved east to Borgotaro and led attacks on the railway line for 10 weeks. On 18 October the captain joined a party of servicemen who were escorted along the Rossano escape line. They crossed to Allied forces a week later. Jack Baddeley received a Mention in Despatches for his actions since leaving the camp.

Lieutenant John Ballantyne from the Royal Armoured Corps served with partisans at Bedonia, but became disillusioned and moved to Cereseto above Bardi. In January 1944 he led three 'other ranks' in a bid to escape north, but they were defeated by heavy snow. The lieutenant became liaison officer with another partisan band. During the enemy summer offensive in the Ceno Valley, he was forced to go into hiding for nine days. Later, John Ballantyne formed a group to collect military intelligence. At the end of October he crossed the 5th Army front. The lieutenant was appointed MBE for his actions.

After leaving PG 49, Lieutenant John (Jack) William Younger of the Coldstream Guards narrowly avoided recapture by hiding in a water tank. Aged 22, he was a Londoner from a titled family, known for his immaculate uniform, languid manner and cigarettes smoked from a long holder.

Jack Younger moved to Mariano with Lieutenant Richard Brooke. As already mentioned, the officers were sheltered by Lazzaro Bazzoni and Ida Papisca and joined a partisan group near Bedonia in January 1944, but became disenchanted following a failed attack.

Lieutenant Younger created an escape line, which successfully evacuated 18 ex-prisoners to Switzerland. One of them travelled as the fireman on the footplate of a railway locomotive. The officer perfected his Italian and collated military information obtained from prisoners and partisans. The intelligence was passed on through rebel channels.

Jack Younger finally commanded a partisan unit for a month, before leaving for liberated territory. He joined SOE agent Lieutenant Commander Adrian Gallegos in a group of nine men and a woman. They reached American forward positions on 20 October. Jack Younger was awarded the MBE for his actions.

In a debriefing report, an SOE interrogator said:

> This officer was with the 31st Garibaldi Brigade in the district of Salsomaggiore, Parma, with HQ at Pellegrino, but had contact also with other brigades in neighbouring districts. He considered that the patriots in this sector (Apennines) are excellent fighting material, providing they have sufficient arms and equipment.
>
> He stated also that although the Garibaldi brigades were generally considered Communist, this was not always the case. A large number of men in the brigade had no or very little Communist feeling. He stated also that the Demo-Christian party has a considerable number of followers amongst the patriots.

Jack Younger returned to England and became an infantry instructor. After the war he served in Germany and Palestine. When on leave in London, Younger met a friend who asked him how he was. 'Furious,' he replied. 'I have just come from Harrods where I was looking for a tie in the menswear department, when a women came up to me and asked: "Are you in gloves?" Certainly not, I told her. I am in the Coldstream Guards!'

After attending Staff College in Camberley in 1949, Jack Younger went back to Italy as Military Attaché at the Embassy in Rome. In 1970 he was promoted to Major General and concluded his military career three years later as Director, Management and Support of Intelligence. In the same year, Jack Younger succeeded as the third baronet.

★

The adjoining province of Piacenza also provided a haven for escapers until the final winter of the war, as recounted in the next chapter. The area even had links with the secret British Organisation in Rome for Assisting Allied Escaped Prisoners of War, which was based over 500 kilometres away to the south.

10

THE OCCUPATION

The remarkable underground organisation for the welfare of Allied escapers and evaders, also known as the Rome Movement, operated for nine months from the September 1943 Armistice to the liberation of the capital on 4 June 1944. It had 3,925 servicemen on its books.

In his wartime memoir, *The Rome Escape Line*, the head of the organisation, Major Sam Derry, wrote that a Royalist Yugoslav officer, Second Lieutenant Cedomir Ristic, had returned from distributing funds in the Arda Valley at Christmastime 1943. Of approximately 600 Allied escapers in the area, about half had made their way to Switzerland or warmer parts of Italy.

The officer reported to Major Derry:

> Owing to the imprudence of prisoners rather than unreliable Italian inhabitants, the police have arrested 18 Italians and offered rewards for information about the source of supply of money for escaped prisoners of war.

Sam Derry wrote: 'This meant disaster for the Italian helpers through the lack of caution of the men they were helping, and I had to think up immediate and drastic steps to tighten security.'

On 15 November 1943 Lieutenant Ristic provided a testimonial to the assistance he had received in the valley from a corn thresher at Lugagnano:

> For English troops: During a dangerous mission of mine in Italy, I was helped by Primo Rebecchi, and therefore I pray the English command to take this into consideration. He was useful in serving me as a guide in reaching the prisoners to whom I had brought the money and information.

Signor Rebecchi also helped Private Thomas Leslie Kenyon, Sherwood Foresters, from Marple in Cheshire, Lieutenant Costas Jacovides, the Cyprus Regiment, and five more officers from the Royal Yugoslav Army. They included Lieutenant Jovan B Grkavac, known to the locals as *Giovanni lo Slavo*, escaped POW from PG 26 Cortemaggiore and commander of the 62nd partisan brigade. He wrote:

> Primo Rebecchi and his family not only sheltered me, but saved my life by keeping me hidden in their house during the savage hunt for Allied prisoners of war on the part of the Nazi-Fascists. Despite the threat of reprisals made by the enemy to those who materially and morally helped the escapers, he exposed himself and his family to danger and showed that he was a true helper of Allied prisoners.

The narrow Piacentine valleys, deciduous woods and quiet countryside created perfect hiding places. The fugitives received spontaneous help from ordinary citizens, local priests and members of the Resistance. In turn, the earliest partisan formations were founded by escapers in a bid to ensure their survival and to avoid recapture.

The *38th Brigata D'Assalto Garibaldi* was set up in the Arda Valley in April 1944 under Lieutenant Giuseppe Prati. It became the *Divisione Valdarda* with 2,193 fighters. There were 350 fatalities. Other formations covered Val Nure, Val Trebbia, Val Tidone and Oltrepò Pavese.

A German garrison housed in the junior school in Castell'Arquato came under sustained fire from partisans on 20 May. Four Fascist strongholds were also attacked by the rebels. According to a militia report, they included numerous Australian ex-prisoners. On 26 May BBC radio announced: 'The flag of freedom is flying over the first liberated commune in occupied Italy' after partisans seized the village of Morfasso at the head of the Arda Valley. The growth of the Resistance movement and the liberation of substantial upland areas by the partisans ensured that the province was the scene of constant change.

During the twenty-month period following the September 1943 Armistice, callers at my family's house at number eight, Via Guglielmo Marconi, Castell'Arquato, included Allied escaped prisoners of war, Italian helpers, German soldiers, their Asian allies, and British and Brazilian troops on the liberation.

In 1998 I was able to obtain copies of Allied Screening Commission files from the United States on the help provided to the prisoners of war by my grandparents, Alfredo and Giuseppina Dall'Arda, and by my mother, Clara. The documents included eight wartime letters from the servicemen. During the war, grandfather had hidden the messages in dark green wine bottles and buried them in the garden at the back of the house.

The POWs had all come from PG 49 Fontanellato and were still in the area at the end of March 1944.

They included:

Lieutenant William Benzie, 42nd Battalion, Royal Tank Regiment, from Glasgow.

Lieutenant John William Burman, 42nd Battalion, Royal Tank Regiment, from Manchester.

Captain Patrick Howard Voltelin de Cleremont, 8th King's Royal Irish Hussars.

Captain John W Fairbrass, 7th Medium Regiment, Royal Artillery, from Colchester.

Lieutenant Charles Hedley, 8th King's Royal Irish Hussars, from Lancashire.

Lieutenant Costas Jacovides, 1002 Pioneer Company, The Cyprus Regiment, from Larnaca, Cyprus.

Captain John Moore, The Leicestershire Regiment.

Private William Leonard Rigby, 1st South African Irish Regiment, Union Defence Force, from Fish Hoek, South Africa.

Sub-Conductor E Victor Rolland, Indian Army Ordnance Corps (IAOC), of French origin.

Lieutenant Kenneth Noel Sutcliffe, Royal Artillery.

Lieutenant John Forrest Taylor, 7th Battalion, Royal Tank Regiment.

Private H John Viljoen, Union Defence Force, from Benoni, Transvaal, South Africa.

Lieutenant André GR Willis, 4th Battalion, 11th Sikh Regiment, Indian Army, from West Moors, Dorset.

Another of the escapers was called Sidney. He was slightly older than the rest, at around 35, well built and of fresh complexion. My mother recalled that the soldier was at the house during a German roundup, a *rastrellamento.* He was very frightened and it was a dangerous situation for everyone, but he was taken into the mountains and made good his escape. After the war Sidney and my mother were able to meet up and reminisce in central London.

*

On the outbreak of war between Britain and Germany in September 1939, my mother took out an international subscription to *Illustrated*, a substantial Odhams magazine which covered the campaign. It arrived regularly by post from London every week, until the issue dated 1 June 1940, when supplies stopped abruptly.

Things looked particularly grim for Great Britain. Holland and Belgium had fallen and the evacuation of the British Expeditionary Force from the Channel ports had begun. Italy declared war on Britain and France on 10 June.

For my relatives this was a terrible shock. Like other pro-British Italians, they found themselves on the wrong side of a war.

After arriving in Italy at age 11, my mother had attended the local primary school for a year, then boarded at the grammar school in Arezzo, before attending the high school in Parma, and finally the apostolic school of Santa Cuore, Albino, Bergamo, run by nuns. Like all pupils, she had to become a member of the Fascist youth movements and take part in synchronised gymnastic displays, parades and the singing of propaganda songs, which she greatly resented.

By the time of the Armistice in September 1943, my mother was a student of Foreign Languages and Literature in her third year at Venice University. She had just turned 23. In this era, most girls remained at home until they were married.

111

The rail journey to and from university was long and dangerous. People packed into the carriages like sardines, even filling the toilet cubicles and the luggage racks. In February 1944 a train taking my mother back to Venice was machine-gunned by Allied aircraft. The driver and fireman were killed. It was becoming too risky to travel between the cities and she had to suspend her studies. In the meantime, there was the chance to give private lessons in foreign languages in the village.

My mother eagerly grasped the unexpected opportunity that had arisen to help the Allied war effort. She took money and items that were rationed or in short supply on the farms to the escaped prisoners of war. After months in the mountains, many of them were in a sorry state. Sometimes they looked like tramps.

As someone born in London, with dual nationality, and a command of several languages, my mother was popular with the escapers. She also acted, in the words of former partisan officer Luigi Sesenna, 'as a point of reference' for other helpers. My mother enjoyed talking with the soldiers about Britain and passing on the latest information gleaned from the illicit broadcasts of Radio London.

Allied aircraft roamed over mountain and plain. On one occasion my mother and her cousin, another Clara, hired bicycles in the village and were travelling up the valley to Lugagnano when they heard the drone of an approaching plane. Only the United States Army Air Force flew by day. Gunfire from their aircraft had already caused several civilian casualties and they had earned the reputation of being trigger-happy.

The plane swooped from behind the hills and began to strafe the narrow road alongside the torrent. Machine gunfire exploded all around them. They only escaped by leaping into the ditch at the side of the road. Mercifully, the aircraft did not turn for another attack. The pair emerged, somewhat dishevelled, but unscathed.

Former partisan officer Oreste Scaglioni recalled my mother's activities at this time:

> I remember your mother well as a tall and strong young girl. Heedless of the danger, she left Castell'Arquato every day with a knapsack, bringing food, clothing and information for the escapers. They were being sheltered in farmhouses in the Vigoleno area, between the Ongina and the Stirone.
>
> She directed the men towards Bardi, where other families who had lived in England would assist them and arrange with Don Guido Anelli and other local clergymen for their escape to Allied lines.

When we first met, Oreste told me: 'Your mother could easily have been shot. There were many Fascists in the village and there was always the risk from spies and informers.' In a dictatorship you can even fear your neighbours. Castell'Arquato had a German headquarters and barracks and Italian infantrymen and *Carabinieri*. Radio and newspapers churned out daily propaganda against those they called 'the traitors of 8 September' and warned of the approaching Communist menace. Film shows, dances and meetings were banned and there was an evening curfew. Identity cards had to be obtained from the town hall for moving between villages.

The journey to the Stirone Valley on foot takes about three hours in each direction. The route was known as the partisan's road as it was taken by so many young men leaving their families to follow the rebel cause.

The itinerary begins by crossing the bridge over the

Arda torrent and following the right bank upstream to the hamlet of Pallastrelli. Country trails lead over the hills facing Castell'Arquato into the little valley of the Ongina. After passing through vineyards and new plantings around the village of Bacedasco, the path climbs another escarpment and finally takes you down into the Stirone Valley.

On one occasion, my mother recalled finding a room full of excitable Polish escaped prisoners of war in one of the houses in La Trinità. They sang the most beautiful songs and she was able to speak to some of them in French. Only the silver light of dawn on the facing hills alerted my mother that it was time to leave.

As well as being dangerous and illegal, supplying the escapers was no simple matter. Rationing had been introduced in Italy in 1941 owing to the Allied naval blockade, but after two or three years even basics were only available on the black market or through barter.

Self-help and improvisation were the order of the day. Soap was made at home using crystals of caustic soda (sodium hydroxide), animal fat and water. The process was lengthy and sometimes hazardous, but did produce nice mild bars of white soap.

With clothing, it was a case of make do and mend. A local dressmaker would call at the houses and in two or three days make new garments out of old. They were unpicked, turned inside out and re-stitched.

Clothing was in constant demand by the escapers, especially as it was often wet and cold in the mountains. My grandfather sent a suit, jackets, shirts and trousers. Grandmother would spin sheep's wool on a handloom and dye the yarn. She and my mother used it to knit pullovers, scarves, hats, underwear, socks and gloves for the men. They also made them handkerchiefs by cutting and hemming cotton sheets. The escapers were also provided with money and cigarettes, toothpaste, books, wine and shoes.

Goods made from leather were scarce. At the beginning of the war a pair of shoes could be bought for five lire. Later they cost five thousand. One pretty pair my mother bought fell apart in the rain. The sole had been made out of compressed cardboard and dyed. In the summer, most people wore wooden mules with webbing. The girls carried hammers and nails in their bags to carry out repairs. Luckily, a helper was found who had access to a store of boots that could be given to the escapers, as we shall see.

Owing to the absence of imports, sugar had to be replaced by honey, or by sugar beet that was grown in local fields and boiled into a syrup. Chicory was used instead of coffee. An infusion of lime flowers became a substitute for tea. My mother particularly missed chocolate. Fortunately, on the liberation the Allied troops had plentiful supplies of all the items that the Italians had been starved of for years. The Americans were especially generous.

Any goods that my family could not obtain for the escapers from the farm or the home were purchased from a shop known as the *appalto*. It was just above the arch in the old walls at the bottom of the village. The store was licensed by the government to sell salt, tobacco, and tax stamps, and also stocked a wide variety of everyday necessities. My grandfather smoked a pipe and *Toscano* cigars, so my mother's purchase of smoker's items requested by the men did not arouse suspicion.

The young partisan Oreste Scaglioni noticed my mother's trips into the countryside to help escapers, but most people did not. Walking was the usual way of moving around. Only a few people owned a car, such as the mayor, doctor and vet. The roads were built for mule or horse and cart and had not yet been asphalted. This was still true of the track to the farm when we visited in 1958. Our car left a plume of grey-white dust in its wake.

*

We have looked at the successful escapes of several of the soldiers helped by my family: Captain Patrick de Cleremont and lieutenants William Benzie, John Burman, Charles Hedley, Kenneth Sutcliffe and John Taylor. This is what happened to the others.

The two privates, Rigby and Viljoen, were amongst the 37 South African orderlies at PG 49 out of a pool of 46. They had all volunteered for the role when in other camps, eager to share what they were sure would be the high degree of comfort enjoyed by the officers.

Driver William Leonard Rigby came from Ivordor, 1st Avenue in the municipality of Fish Hoek, now part of Cape Town. He was born in 1907, worked as a bus driver and enlisted in the Union Defence Force in 1940 at age 32. The private served in the 1st South African Irish Regiment of the 1st Infantry Division and was captured at Sidi Rezegh in Libya. Before PG 49 he had been held on the coast at PG 52 Chiavari in Liguria.

William Rigby related: 'I escaped from Fontanellato on 9 September 1943 after the Armistice. I was recaptured on 29 April 1944 in the Parma district by the Fascists.' He was sent to *Stalag* 8D at Teschen, which was then in Upper Silesia in Poland. It is now divided into two towns, Cieszyn in Poland and Český Těšín in the Czech Republic. From June to November 1944 the driver mined coal at work camp E579 at Niwka.

As the end of the war approached, the prisoners and their guards made the dangerous march to link up with British and American forces in face of the advancing Russians, who reached Teschen on 17 March 1945.

William Rigby's companion, Private H John Viljoen, was from the Transvaal, home address: 19c, Fort Steet, Benoni. Following his recapture at the end of April 1944 he was held in *Stalag* 7A Moosburg in Bavaria, Germany's largest POW camp.

A letter from the 'other ranks' escapers to my mother when they were at La Trinità (written by Private Viljoen) reads:

Dear Miss,

We thank you very much for the shirt and the pair of pants which we have received from you. It is very nice to think that there are still people here in Italy that really care for the English. We hope that if God spares our lives that we might return this great favour you have done for us.

Giovanni
Leonardo

P.S. Mary [Dolci] told us that if we need anything we must write and ask you. We need these things:

Two shirts, two hats, two pairs socks, soap, handkerchiefs, cigarettes, two jackets, toothpaste and brushes. These are all the articles we need, if they can be found.

Three of the officers were recaptured. Lieutenant André GR Willis served in the 4th Battalion of the 11th Sikh Regiment. It was the most highly decorated unit in the Indian Army and fought in the Middle East, North Africa and Italy.

The lieutenant was imprisoned at *Stalag* 7A Moosburg. So too was Captain John Moore of the Leicestershire Regiment. Captain John W Fairbrass from the Medium Regiment of the Royal Artillery was held in *Oflag* 7B Eichstätt, which was also in Barvaria.

Another officer, Costas Jacovides, was a Greek Cypriot from Larnaca. He was promoted to full lieutenant at PG 41 Montalbo before coming to PG 49. The officer served in 1002 Pioneer Company of the Cyprus Regiment, which was raised as part of the British Army in 1940 and disbanded in 1950.

When the encampment on the Rovacchia broke up, Lieutenant Jacovides volunteered to work on a local farm, together with his friend from Montalbo, Second Lieutenant William John (Jack) Frank Clarke of the Royal Army Ordnance Corps. The first holding was not to their liking, so they went to lodge with the local district nurse, Signorina Bianca Gelati, until she found them a new billet. It was the farm of the Gotti family at Cannètolo, a little hamlet to the west of Fontanellato.

The officers stayed from 16 to 27 September, helping the farmers to harvest beetroot and Indian Corn. German raids on surrounding farms prompted Jack Clarke to decide to leave the area. In contrast, Costas Jacovides wanted to remain and wait for the British to arrive.

Jack Clarke found two new companions, the Fontanellato dentist, South African captain Marcus Kane-Burman, and one of his acting technicians, a Royal Navy Able Seaman, A McLean. They began the long trek south.

The trio were recaptured within sight of Allied positions on the River Sangro on 19 November. The officers managed to jump from a prison train near Orte on 5 December, but became separated. After many further adventures, Jack Clarke escaped to Switzerland on 24 February 1944, together with fellow forty-niners, Lieutenant Anthony Laing, Royal

Engineers, and Captain Ted Mumford, 3rd Gurkha Rifles.

Captain Kane-Burman was recaptured in Rome on 8 January, but escaped from another prison train as it crossed into Lombardy. On 1 March he also reached Switzerland. The captain became Chief Dental Officer to the large Allied escaper and evader community interned in the Confederation. On 1 March 1945 he was appointed MBE for services to his fellow prisoners of war in Italy.

Lieutenant Jacovides adopted the alias of *Mario* and moved to the Arda Valley. He was helped by several residents of Castell'Arquato and by Angelo Istroni and family three miles higher up the valley in Lugagnano. They also owned a mill (now derelict) on the right bank of the Arda torrent, near the hamlet of Pallastrelli, half way to Castell'Arquato.

One of Angelo's granddaughters, Silvana Ghezzi, told me:

> *Mario* stayed at the textile mill that belonged to the family of my maternal grandmother. When it became too dangerous a hiding place, both for him and the *mezzadri* who had looked after him, my family decided that he would be safer at my grandmother's house in town. She lived in Lugagnano, in Via Matteotti, a few paces from the *Carabiniere* barracks. *Mario* always wrote to my aunt Adriana, who, I am told, was then an attractive 17-year-old, of whom he had become fond. But the person who looked after his safety was my mother Livia Istroni. Among other things, she was a partisan courier under the name of *Katusha*.

Lieutenant Jacovides's helpers in Castell'Arquato included Signora Alba Sebastiani. A blonde high school gymnastics mistress, aged 30, she was a widow, with a three-year-old son called Franco.

In 1938 the teacher had married naval lieutenant Agostino Angeloni, a submariner from Genoa. They made their home in La Spezia, but when the lieutenant was lost on active service, Alba returned to her home village with their son. The house was number 130 on Via Sforza Caolzio, the small road that winds to the top of Castell'Arquato. The teacher recalled that Lieutenant Jacovides arrived at Christmastime in 1943 and stayed for a total of 10 days in 2 visits.

Over the next eight months Alba also took the officer items when he was at the mill at Pallastrelli. They included woollen pyjamas, an elegant shirt and an angora pullover, cigarettes, butter, wine, liquors, cakes, honey, tea, sugar and bars of soap. She added: 'I also helped the lieutenant by placing myself in danger to ensure that he was not captured. I accompanied him whenever he had to go out, as the authorities were looking for him.'

After leaving the teacher's home, Costas Jacovides came to stay with my family for 10 days at the house in Via Guglielmo Marconi. On 17 January he wrote a letter to Alba saying that he had to leave on the orders of a Signora Scaglioni. He asked for help for two or three days till he found out more about conditions at Lugagnano.

Signora Emma Pollorsi, a retired primary school teacher, and a teenager in wartime, related that Lieutenant Jacovides came to lodge with her and her mother, Filomena, for about a month. They were also hiding an Italian soldier. The house at 12, Vicolo San Pietro, is in a little lane on the hill in the oldest part of Castell'Arquato.

She recalled:

> He often showed me a photograph of a lady with a baby who he said was his sister. He also talked about Cyprus, and spoke Italian well. As long as he remained with us, he was treated as one of the family.

Eventually, it became too dangerous for Lieutenant Jacovides to remain in Lugagnano. The barracks was hit by fire and the wall of the neighbouring Istroni house developed large cracks. In September 1944 Livia took 'Mario' to a new refuge in Castelletto, a small village beyond the dam on the Arda at Mignano. A note to Adriana from Lieutenant Jacovides on 25 October said that he was leaving for the Pelizzone Pass, where he would rendezvous with three other prisoners of war. Their escape through the lines was under way.

The president of the Cyprus Veterans' Association WWII, Mr Loizos Demetriou, told me: 'On his return to Cyprus, Costas Jacovides rejoined the Cyprus Regiment and served until the end of the war, reaching the rank of major. After his discharge from the Army he lived and worked in his hometown of Larnaca.'

Signora Filomena Scaglioni was a benefactor of the prisoners and partisans. She lived in a flat on the second floor of the block overlooking the market square at the bottom of the village. It was 80 yards from the primary school being used as the German barracks. Every few days, my mother and Pietro Guarnieri would call on Filomena, a lively well-to-do lady, daughter of an elderly shoe factory owner and widow of Signor Marchi. Over a glass or two of cherry brandy, the trio would discuss their plans to help the escapers.

One of the former prisoners of war, the Yugoslav lieutenant and partisan commander Jovan B Grkavac, recalled: 'Filomena freely gave clothes, boots, money and food to whoever asked for them.' The assistance was provided in a large area between Castell'Arquato and Lugagnano where there were very many escapers. Amongst those who received help were 'Captain *Patrizio* de Cleremont and his group of English POWs,' Prince Don Alfonso de Liguori, who was a civilian internee with South African nationality, and several fellow Yugoslav officers. Filomena's aid was usually taken to the prisoners in the mountains by Pietro Guarnieri or Signorina Rosa Manzi of Lugagnano.

Filomena Scaglioni's nephews, Oreste and Augusto, were both partisan officers. Their stepfather, Raffaele, was an Italian army lieutenant colonel. He was captured during the German takeover of Parma and deported to a concentration camp. Towards the end of September 1943, his wife Valentina and the two boys became evacuees at the apartment of the paternal grandparents in Castell'Arquato. The flat was in the same block of residential and shop premises as that of Filomena at the bottom of the village. For 10 to 15 days the family hid an escaped prisoner of war, probably 'Mario,' Lieutenant Costas Jacovides.

Oreste was called up by the Fascist Republic in October 1943, but instead left to join the partisans in the mountains. He met the escaped prisoners from Fontanellato who had also taken up arms. In August 1944 Oreste transferred to the Valdarda Division. The following March he was promoted to liaison officer at the zonal command at Groppallo in the Nure Valley. His younger brother, Augusto, aged 19, guided escaped prisoners of war from PG 49 into the mountains after the Armistice and took part in student protests against German occupation. He joined Oreste as a partisan in June under the alias of *Flavio*. Following combat against the Germans during the summer roundup, Augusto was made leader of a new detachment. He fell in action on 4 December at the Pass of Guselli when a column sent to prevent the enemy occupying Morfasso was ambushed.

In the first months of 1945, Signora Scaglioni was obliged to flee the village after threats from the Fascists that she would be shot. At the end of the war, the Allied Screening Commission recommended her to the British War Office for the Award of Commendation (Certificate 17) 'for services rendered to the Allied cause for approximately one year,' but as usual only the Alexander Certificate was granted.

Ten of the 17 British Commonwealth prisoners of war helped by Filomena Scaglioni also received assistance from my family. The others were South Africans: Lance Bombardier HC Van Biljon and Private J Freedman, and Britons: Driver G Bicknell, Royal Army Service Corps; Private Thomas Leslie Kenyon, Sherwood Foresters; Guardsman J Dinsmore, Irish Guards; Trooper John Harrison, Royal Armoured Corps; and Lieutenant R Selby, Bedfordshire and Hertfordshire Regiment.

Private Kenyon and the two South African soldiers were sheltered in Lugagnano until the winter of 1944 and were able to cross the lines. Lieutenant Selby also avoided recapture. In contrast, Driver Bicknell was arrested and sent to *Stalag* 11A Altengrabow, while Guardsman Dinsmore and Trooper Harrison were casualties of war.

*

The departure of many of the POWs along escape lines in late 1944 was fortunate timing. In a radio proclamation on 10 November, General Alexander said that owing to the weather the Allies would launch no major attack until the spring. The partisans were to cease from engaging in large-scale operations, conserve all stores of ammunition and await further orders.

The directive was a great set back for the Resistance and a tonic for their enemies, as we shall see in the next chapter. The partisans had nowhere to go.

11

THE BATTLE OF THE SNOW

German and Fascist leaders viewed General Alexander's proclamation to the Resistance in November 1944 as an invitation to launch attacks on partisan-held areas across occupied Italy. At the end of the month they invaded the Apennine valleys.

The force consisted of three regiments of the new Italian *Bersaglieri* Division and 5,000 legionaries from the German 162nd Infantry Division, often known to the Allies as the 'Turkoman Division.' It was the largest of Hitler's Eastern Volunteer Formations, created from captured Soviet prisoners of war and refugees. The unit was led by German officers but composed of Turkmen and Azerbaijanis. They were always called *i mongoli*, or the Mongols, by the Italians.

The troops overran the partisans in three of the four main Piacentine valleys, the Tidone, Trebbia and Nure. They had made a rapid advance of almost 100 kilometres from across the plain, but stopped suddenly on the edge of the Arda Valley in the south of the province.

The War Diary of the German 14th Army reveals the reason. The 162nd Division met such stubborn resistance between

23 November and 2 December that many detachments needed reorganising owing to heavy losses.

Over the next five days the Valdarda partisans also conducted successful counter-attacks at the entrances to the valley, with the help of some fighters from the Nure. The enemy were forced to halt on their positions for a month.

In early 1945 the offensive resumed. On Twelfth Night, when snow was three feet deep, a force of 15,000 Italian and Asian troops launched the largest ever roundup in the border area. The republican forces included the *Bersaglieri, Littorio* and *Decima Mas* divisions, as well as the Black Brigades and the Italian SS.

It was the first time that villagers had seen the Mongols, as my mother related:

> It was New Year and there was heavy snow. I was with my mother and father in one of the fields just along the road past our house. The farmer had said that we could gather some sugar beet, which we used to make our sweetener.
>
> Suddenly, a long column of Mongol troops began to emerge through the gloom. They had come from the Vigolo Marchese direction and were going into the village. The soldiers rode on horses and sledges and wore furs. They had inscrutable expressions and long moustaches. It was like a scene from the Russian steppe.
>
> Before long, the Mongols began to call at our house, looking for food and drink. I think they were based just around the corner at the San Carlo inn.
>
> My father was hospitable to everyone, so once the soldiers had shown that they were no threat to us, he made them welcome too. Fortunately, we had

plenty of provisions from the farm. As usual, the wine flowed freely.

The Mongols gained a fearsome reputation when fighting the partisans, but we found them gentle, almost child-like. They said my father was their father, my mother was their mother, and that I was their sister.

German soldiers were imposed as lodgers on local families. The troops were said to be part of work detachments based at the local airport of San Damiano, which was increasingly coming under attack by Allied aircraft.

My mother recalled:

We were very alarmed when the soldiers hammered on our door. But they made it clear that they only wanted rooms. On the whole, the Germans acted in a proper manner and got on with their own affairs. They did not take any of our food, for example. It was said that the men were well behaved because their headquarters was in the village.

The troops were pleased to discover that I spoke German and I used to converse with one or two of them. I remember that one day they wanted more space and were keen to take over my room. The NCO in charge said to me: 'Young lady, you must go and sleep with your mother and father.' But I told him that I would not. After a few moments, he shrugged and walked off and the matter was never mentioned again.

The Germans occupied the main room, the *sala,* on the ground floor. I could not stop thinking of the escapers sitting on the settee talking to us there only a few weeks earlier.

We were very pleased when the Germans went after about six weeks. The *sala* had a fine marble tile floor and hand decorated gold leaf on the walls. We discovered that the soldiers had caused some damage and kept rabbits in the room to supplement their rations.

Several people said that the Germans staying in Castell'Arquato were not too bad. Many were conscripts and seemed to be courteous and intelligent enough.

But a youth from the village who went to Venice University with me was executed by German troops for no reason. His family were not allowed to bury his body. We also lost one of my second cousins, a young partisan fighter.

After the mighty enemy roundup, the partisans resumed their activities in the middle of February 1945, reinforced by British SOE and American OSS missions. On Thursday, 5 April a column of German and Fascist troops launched a dawn attack on Castell'Arquato with the intention of demolishing the bridge over the Arda and severing links to Fiorenzuola and the Via Emilia.

As soldiers began to lay charges under the arches, they were hit from several different directions by fire from partisans of the 38th and 62nd brigades, armed with mortars, machine guns and light weapons.

The saboteurs abandoned their dynamite and the column splintered. Fighting spread along Via Guglielmo Marconi and into the garden of my grandparents' home.

As bullets began to ricochet off the walls of the house, my grandfather boiled olive oil on the gas stove to throw over any of the Germans rash enough to enter. Fortunately for both parties, none tried. The partisans captured two armoured cars and took many prisoners that day. The bullet holes left in the window shutters of the house impressed me a great deal as a boy.

The Allied offensive resumed and culminated in the Battle for the River Po. On Saturday, 21 April the 5th Army liberated Bologna, the capital of Emilia. German forces had fled from Fontanellato three days earlier.

The advancing troops reached Parma on the evening of Wednesday, 25 April. Next day the 62nd Brigade of the Valdarda partisan division made contact with the United States 93rd Division at Alseno. German troops scrambled to cross the river. Almost a million were forced to surrender.

My mother and her friends walked to Fiorenzuola to join jubilant crowds cheering the Allied troops as tanks and infantry advanced north along the Via Emilia. The girls threw flowers to the soldiers and gave them bottles of wine.

British and American forces took the city of Piacenza, assisted by the partisan formations of the valleys, on Saturday, 28 April.

All German and Fascist forces in Italy surrendered on Wednesday, 2 May 1945 following 20 months of war in the country. The celebrations began.

As a result of the help they received, more than 15,000 Allied escapers and evaders had crossed the lines within Italy and over 5,000 had reached Switzerland. A few former prisoners of war emerged from their hiding places in the more remote parts of the Italian countryside. Almost 2,000 men were still officially unaccounted for in 1947.

*

An awards bureau for Italian helpers was created as early as 11 July 1944, only 37 days after the liberation of Rome.

The Allied Screening Commission (ASC) was 'responsible for giving recognition to, and compensating, persons in Italy who had assisted Allied personnel behind enemy lines following the Allied armistice with Italy on 3 September 1943.'

The ASC was able to emerge so quickly because it took over the offices and staff of the remarkable British Organisation in Rome for Assisting Allied Escaped Prisoners of War. The bureau's first commanding officer was the youthful Major William Simpson, a Glaswegian former prisoner of war and one of Major Derry's two main service helpers. In October 1945 Major Simpson was succeeded by Lieutenant Colonel Hugo de Burgh.

When all the claims had been processed at the end of the war, ceremonies were held across the peninsula. Representatives of the ASC expressed official thanks and awarded bilingual certificates of merit and cash reimbursements of expenses.

Over 75,000 'Alexander Certificates' were given. Only one was allocated per household. The number of actual helpers was far higher. In addition, as the head was most likely to be a man, the rules meant that the contribution made by women and additional members of the family often remained hidden.

The commission and other service agencies also recommended 447 Italians for additional honours and awards. In December 1947 the British Labour Government rejected their proposals. On 10 April the ASC had closed its doors.

William Simpson left the army in May 1946 and returned to his pre-war employment with the Royal Insurance Company. He related that the reasons given by the Foreign Office for denying such recognition were that it would give offence to British families bereaved at Italian hands, some of those eligible might be Communists and reaction by non-recipients could be counter-productive.

The United States Government did, however, award 17 Medals of Freedom to honour Italian civilians whose actions aided the war effort of the country and its allies. Three of the decorations were for outstanding service.

In his own tribute, William Simpson wrote of the 'Italian men and women who, beyond rational explanation, rose during the Nazi Occupation from submission to heroism without leaving home.'

12

PEACETIME

At the end of the war, the people had to adapt to a new set of rulers, the transitional Allied Military Government (AMG).

The building next to my grandparents' home in Via Guglielmo Marconi in Castell'Arquato, the *Consorzio*, or agricultural cooperative, became the barracks for soldiers of the victorious Brazilian Infantry Division.

My family invited the soldiers to a party to celebrate the liberation. In the front room of the house there was a handsome veneered Philips radiogram, a combined radio and record player. During the war, my mother used to walk down from the farm on summer evenings to listen to the latest news on the fighting from Radio London, and return after midnight. Now the radiogram was used to play records to accompany the Foxtrot. It must have been a good party, because friends and relatives still remember it today.

My mother decided to volunteer to work for the Allied Military Government and called at the provincial headquarters, which was located in the Gothic Palace in the centre of Piacenza. After a short interview she was employed as the interpreter for the Governor, a very pleasant American,

Major Lewis J McIntyre.

While lodging in the city my mother met her future husband, my father, Kenneth Winston Tudor, from Newtown, Montgomeryshire, in Mid-Wales, who arrived with the liberating 8th Army. He was a regular soldier in the Royal Corps of Signals and veteran of the evacuation of the British Expeditionary Force from the French Channel ports in 1940. There too the order had been given: 'Every man for himself.'

On 14 June 1943 my father had embarked at Greenock on the SS Ascania for the voyage to North Africa. In July, he was in the invasion force that came ashore from tank landing craft at Portopalo on Cape Passero in Sicily.

Two years later, my father was one of four sergeants in the Sixteen-Line Section of the Royal Signals. He was 26 years old. The unit consisted of about 65 men, who were split into small detachments. They worked alongside various other Commonwealth nationalities and Poles and Americans. The immediate task at the end of the war was to replace the telephone wires along the portion of main railway line from Piacenza to Parma, which had been destroyed by Allied bombing.

At the end of 1945, my mother invited my father and his close friends from the corps, signalmen Hugh (Hugo) Rees and William (Bill) Hannon, to stay with the family for an English-style Christmas. My mother bought glass baubles and trimmings for the tree in Piacenza.

Hugo, from Llanelli, in peacetime a stable lad, was aged 22 at the time. He told me: 'Your grandfather was a big, jovial man and he treated us all like part of the family. He was so kind to us. We hadn't had a home Christmas for three or four years. But it was all over in a couple of days, sad to say.'

My father completed his continental army service with British-Troops-in-Austria (BTA) as the Quartermaster

Sergeant of the 3rd Railway Telegraph Squadron at Villach. He returned to civilian life on 4 May 1947 following more than eight years with the Colours. With another four years in the reserve, my father became a rural postman and then a linesman and foreman with Post Office Telephones.

Once the AMG ceased operations in December 1945, my mother returned to Venice University. Over the next year and a half she trained as a teacher and also worked in Rome as the secretary of Italian army colonel Alberto Inzani, her first cousin once removed. Aged about 60, he was a landowner, an engineer by profession, originally from Vernasca.

After my father left the army in 1947, my mother returned to her beloved London following an absence of 16 years. Her mother and father gave her the money for the fare from the remuneration received from the Allied Screening Commission for expenses in helping the prisoners of war. She found employment as the governess to a doctor's children. My parents married in Swindon, Wiltshire, in February 1948 and moved to Mid-Wales.

Grandfather Alfredo never returned to London. Foreign travel was far less common in those days (except for reasons of war or economic necessity) and he was very happy with life in the village.

In contrast, in later years, grandmother Giuseppina made regular trips to Mid-Wales to see her daughter, son-in-law and the two grandchildren: me and my sister, Monica. In the early 1960s grandmother came to live with us at our home, Breeze Hill, in Newtown.

The house on Via Guglielmo Marconi in Castell'Arquato was sold, as was the farm *Bertacca*. With the abolition of the *mezzadria* system in 1964 many such holdings became uneconomic for their owners. A traditional way of life was lost forever.

Over the next few years, grandmother bought a flat in Castell'Arquato for occasional visits and two more as investments, one in Fiorenzuola and the other on the coast at Imperia. But gradually the capital dwindled and finally the decision was made to sell everything.

After countless generations of Italian forbears, my family turned into occasional visitors and no longer residents. Fortunately, by now we were entering the age of modern communications. I became the family historian, celebrating an Anglo-Italian heritage spanning a century of continuity and change, war and peace, migration and romance. It was a short step from writing about the British and South African escapers my family helped to covering the whole prisoner of war experience.

*

Over the years, I have visited many of the towns and villages in the Emilian countryside whose people showed such solidarity with Allied escaped prisoners of war and downed airmen.

The former camp at Fontanellato, PG 49, is now the Centro Cardinal Ferrari, a specialist private hospital. It is named after a famous local priest, Andrea Ferrari, who became Cardinal Archbishop of Milan. During the First World War, he sponsored charities in aid of widows and orphans, relatives of servicemen missing in action, and prisoners of war. The cardinal was beatified by Pope John Paul II in 1987.

As we have seen, after the Allied prisoners of war escaped on 9 September 1943, the camp was ransacked by both German troops and Italian civilians. Later, the building was used as a school for officer cadets of the Fascist republic, the RSI. At the same time, the Rocca Sanvitale, the moated castle in the village centre, was a German Headquarters.

As a result of these strategic targets, Fontanellato was hit several times by Allied bombers.

In 1948 the Children's Home of the Madonna of Fontanellato finally opened. At its peak it housed 250 orphans and 23 sisters, about half of its complement of prisoners of war. The orphanage closed in 1982 when new regional arrangements were made.

On my first visit to the former camp in the summer of 2000, I found that the building was as large and impressive as I had expected. It was not hard to imagine hundreds of prisoners of war forming up in the courtyard for roll call.

On railings to the left of the main gateway there is a metal panel, which reads:

> This plaque records, on the fortieth anniversary, the British and Allied prisoners of war who were interned here in prison camp PG 49 [and] the people of Fontanellato who after the Armistice of 8 September 1943 helped and hid them at the risk of severe reprisals.
>
> Fontanellato, 11 September 1983.

What happened to the more than 500 officers and men who marched out of the camp at midday on 9 September 1943?

The first United States officer sent to help with official rescue work in the south of Italy, Captain Richard Lewis, commented in October of the same year: 'The opportunity of rescuing really large numbers of prisoners had already been lost when the Armistice was announced.' There were always going to be far more recaptures than successful escapes.

So it was at Fontanellato. The majority of the prisoners were eventually rounded up and sent to camps in Greater Germany. They remained behind the wire until liberated at the end of the war in May 1945.

As for the rest of the servicemen, some were shot by Germans and Fascists. Others perished in severe weather. A few were never heard of again. Amongst the missing were the authors of *The Cage*, lieutenants Dan Billany and David Dowie. They had left their manuscript with the Meletti farming family at Soragna, who sent it to Billany's parents in the spring of 1946. The book was first published in 1949 with a note that the fate of the authors was unknown. Recent evidence suggests that they perished high in the Apennines late in 1943, together with another escaper from PG 49, Lieutenant Alec Harding, Royal Artillery.

Perhaps as many as a fifth of the forty-niners were successful escapers. They were divided roughly equally between those who reached Switzerland and the rest who crossed Allied lines within Italy. I am proud that my family helped some of the men on their way.

After visiting the former camp for the first time, I followed the route taken by many of the escapers after the Armistice. To the Stirone, which meanders towards the plain at Fidenza. To rolling hills and oak and chestnut woods. To the little villages of La Villa, La Trinità and Borla, which hug the curves of the country road. To farms with two-tiered barns, where the hay had already been gathered in. To paths across the mountains. To freedom.

BIBLIOGRAPHY

Aimi, Amos, and Copelli, Aldo, *Fidenza nella Resistenza*, Fidenza: Collana Storica Fidentina, 1984.

Barker, Arthur James, *Prisoners of War*, New York: Universe Books, 1975.

Billany, Dan, in collaboration with Dowie, David, *The Cage*, London: Longmans, 1949.

Churchill, Winston S, *The Second World War, Volume V, Closing the Ring*, London: Book Club Associates, 1987.

Comyn, John Andrew, *Episodes*, private circulation, 1994.

Davies, Tony, *When the Moon Rises, An Escape through Wartime Italy*, London: Sphere Books, 1988.

De Burgh, Hugo, *Oldtown, the House and its People*, privately published, 2007.

Derry, Sam, *The Rome Escape Line*, London: Harrap, 1960.

English, Ian (ed.), *Home by Christmas?* Privately published, 1997.

Graham, Dominick, *The Escapes and Evasions of 'An Obstinate Bastard,'* York: Wilton 65, 2000.

Kindersley, the Hon. Philip, *For You the War is Over*, Tunbridge Wells: Midas Books, 1983.

Lamb, Richard, *War in Italy 1943-1945, A Brutal Story*, Harmondsworth: Penguin Books, 1995.

Langrishe, John, *The Long Walk Out, or Home for Christmas*, private circulation, 1994.

Lewin, Ronald, *Rommel as Military Commander*, New York: Barnes and Noble, 1968.

Minardi, Marco, *L'Orizzonte del Campo*, Fidenza: Casa Editrice Mattioli, 1995.

Newby, Eric, *Love and War in the Apennines*, London: Pan Books, 1983.

Newby, Wanda, *Peace and War, Growing up in Fascist Italy*, London: Collins, 1991.

Prati, Giuseppe, *La Resistenza in Val d'Arda*, Piacenza: Casa Editrice Vicolo del Pavone, 1994.

Ross, Michael, *From Liguria with Love*, London: Minerva Press, 1997.

Rossiter, Jack, *'You'll Never Make It,' The Escape Diary of Pte. Jack Rossiter, August-September 1943*, Cirencester: Englang Publishing, 1992.

Scaglioni, Oreste, *Memorie di vita Partigiana fra la Val Ceno e la Valdarda*, private circulation, n.d.

Scaglioni, Oreste, *Rime sulla Val d'Arda Partigiana*, private circulation, n.d.

Simpson, William, *A Vatican Lifeline '44*, London: Leo Cooper, 1995.

Tudor, Malcolm, *At War in Italy 1943-1945: True Adventures in Enemy Territory*, Newtown: Emilia Publishing, 2007.

Tudor, Malcolm, *Beyond the Wire: A True Story of Allied POWs in Italy 1943-1945*, Newtown: Emilia Publishing, 2009.

Tudor, Malcolm, *Escape from Italy 1943-45: Allied Escapers and Helpers in Fascist* Italy, Newtown: Emilia Publishing, 2003.

Tudor, Malcolm, *Prisoners and Partisans: Escape and Evasion in World War II Italy*, Newtown: Emilia Publishing, 2006.

Tudor, Malcolm, *SOE in Italy 1940-1945: The Real Story*, Newtown: Emilia Publishing, 2011.

Tudor, Malcolm, *Special Force: SOE and the Italian Resistance 1943-1945*, Newtown: Emilia Publishing, 2004.

INDEX OF NAMES